asian bites

asian bites

A feast of flavours from Turkey through India to Japan

Tom Kime

Photography by Lisa Linder

London New York Munich
Melbourne Delhi

Thanks go to my wife, Kylie Burgess Kime, for her ongoing love and support of our great life, and for being such an enthusiastic travel companion. To my mother, Helen, for being the inspiration behind my love of food; to my father, Robert, for igniting my love of travel and discovery; and to my sister, Hannah, for her ongoing curiosity and encouragement to pursue my goals. To my godchildren Frank, Alice, and Raphael, with whom I look forward to sharing many meals. To everyone who loves food and travel.

Project Manager and Editor
Siobhán O'Connor

Managing Editor
Dawn Henderson

Photographic Art Direction and Design
Simon Daley

Senior Art Editor
Susan Downing

Food and Author Photography
Lisa Linder

Editorial Assistant
Ariane Durkin

Food Stylist
Alice Hart

Production Editor
Jenny Woodcock

Prop Stylist
Rachel Jukes

Production Controller
Mandy Inness

First published in Great Britain in 2008 by Dorling Kindersley Limited
80 Strand, London WC2R 0RL

Penguin Group (UK)

Copyright © 2008 Dorling Kindersley
Text copyright © 2008 Tom Kime

2 4 6 8 10 9 7 5 3 1

A CIP catalogue record for this book is available from the British Library

ISBN: 978 1 4053 1961 4

Colour reproduction by MDP, United Kingdom
Printed and bound in China by Leo Paper Group

Discover more at
www.dk.com

Contents

Carrot pachadi | Korean hot pickled cabbage | Spiced stuffed
aubergine | Laotian spice-pickled spring onions | Sichuan peppered
beef | Lemon and saffron chicken kebabs | Potato with turmeric
and mustard seeds | **Keynotes** Citrus and lemongrass | Fried
aubergine with toasted sesame seeds | Tomato chutney with
green chilli | Tamarind beef with peanuts

Introduction

It is often said that Asian people are always eating. There seem to be so many opportunities to eat at any time of the day or night. For a chef and writer that makes Asia a perfect place to travel and sample the wares. Ever present throughout the vastly different countries and cuisines of Asia, with its many hundreds of ethnic groups, is a healthy obsession with food. The constant grazing on freshly cooked delights means that you experience a vast wealth of flavours, textures, and fabulous taste combinations. These in turn create layers and three-dimensional tastes that form delicious food. This depth of flavour creates subtleties, contrast, and nuance, so that no one ingredient stands out, overpowering the meal.

This same description can be applied to the cultures of Asian countries. Asia is full of blends of

> "Asia is full of blends of people, beliefs, and religion, with layers of migration, conquest, and history that work to highlight, complement, and contrast, forming countries that have a wealth and depth of heritage."

people, beliefs, and religion, with layers of migration, conquest, and history that work to highlight, complement, and contrast, forming countries that have a wealth and depth of heritage. This layering becomes even more interesting because, across the vast continent of Asia, it is impossible to separate the connection of food and society. The style of food differs enormously from region to region, and the ingredients and recipes change, but the significance of the food remains constant. The food of Asia is an integral part of life. I refer to this as the "anthropology of food", and it makes the connection between food and travel in regions of Asia so enjoyable.

For example, the significance of rice throughout Asia goes much further than as a food staple. How it is cooked is paramount to the success of an Asian meal. Rice is a cultural cornerstone in many ancient heritages that have formed over millennia across a land that covers thousands of miles. The importance of rice lies not only in the food and eating etiquette, but also in the society as a whole: the art, literature, music, religion, spiritual superstitions, economics, and politics of this vast continent. In many Asian cultures, the food that is eaten becomes a meal when eaten alongside rice; without it, the same food would just be a snack. In China, the phrase *chi fan* ("to eat rice") also translates as "to eat". In Thailand and Vietnam, there are scores of phrases that use rice to describe aspects of society, such as generosity, love, and waiting a long time for something to happen – referring to the cultivation of rice. In Thailand, the word for rice is *khao*; a common term of greeting is "Kin khao laew reu yang?" ("Have you consumed rice yet?"). Another common greeting in Asia translates roughly as, "Hi, there. You must be hungry." When greeted in this manner, I cannot help but accept the generous offer of more food, even if I have only just eaten.

The use of chilli is now synonymous with many Asian cuisines, and it would be hard to imagine the foods of Thailand, India, and Malaysia without this

fiery condiment. Yet it was only after the Portuguese and Spanish had been to South America in the 16th century that Asia adopted the chilli into its cuisine. Before the arrival of this heated fruit, however, many of these cuisines were already hot and spicy. Pastes of ginger, garlic, and pepper were used, along with

"It was only after the Portuguese and Spanish had been to South America in the 16th century that Asia adopted the chilli into its cuisine. Before the arrival of this heated fruit, however, many of these cuisines were already hot and spicy. Pastes of ginger, garlic, and pepper were used, along with other spices."

other spices. White pepper was particularly favoured in Thai cooking, to provide a serious kick. Thai dishes that use white pepper are quite likely to be ancient Siamese recipes predating the Spanish arrival with their hot spoils from South America.

Images of Asia and its varied cuisines are steeped in mystique and intrigue that go back millennia. The sensual delights and aromas of the cuisines of Asia and the Orient are evocative of ancient trade routes, exotic spice markets, and centuries of secrets that have transfixed everyone before me who has come into contact with them – including the Romans, who have been documented as using spice blends of cumin and ginger. In Roman cuisine, salty anchovy pastes were used to season dishes in a similar fashion to the way Asian fish sauce and dried and fermented shrimp have been used in Southeast and East Asia for thousands of years.

I am fascinated by the use of spices in Asian cooking, and these extraordinary aromatic seeds and pods from far-distant Asian lands have held outsiders in a spell over many different eras. In England in the 16th and 17th centuries, nutmeg was widely used for many reasons, both medicinal and culinary, because of its taste and strong antibacterial and preservative qualities, but most importantly because it was said to ward off the plague. The Arabs controlled the precious spice trade, and the spice islands of Indonesia were so valuable that individual sultans amassed great wealth. By the early 1500s, Maluku (or the Moluccas, famous for cloves and nutmeg) was known as Jazirat-al-Muluk, or "Land of Many Kings". Later these islands were crucial in shaping Western history. In the 18th century, at the end of the Second Anglo-Dutch War, the Dutch gained control of Run island in Indonesia's Moluccan archipelago, in exchange for British control of New Amsterdam (Manhattan, New York).

In Asian cooking, there should be a perfect balance of tastes between hot, sweet, salty, and sour. In Thailand, this is called *rot chart*, or "correct taste". This balance is achieved through the use of spices, pepper, chilli, fresh herbs, citrus, and salty elements made from fermenting and dried soya and seafood products. The wide use of fresh herbs right across Asia distinctly marks its cuisines with an aromatic freshness. All these fresh herbs are one of the reasons that Vietnamese food, for instance, is described lovingly as "perfumed" or "fragrant".

In Thailand, they do not restrict themselves to the leaves of fresh coriander, but use the roots as well. An analogy is made between a tree with its roots and a bunch of coriander. A tree gains nutrients through its roots; if you were to translate nutrients into flavour, the roots are where most of the intense flavour is, and the leaves have the least because they are farthest away. Fresh coriander roots are a vital element in the making and flavouring of Thai curry pastes, marinades, and spicy dressings.

This balance of Asian flavours is achieved in all types of dishes, from the simplest dipping sauce

"Whenever I am travelling in Asia, I sample so many different dishes of enormous variety, yet you can always trace this simple balance of taste and flavour running through them."

all the way up to royal banquets consisting of many components. What is fascinating is that this blend is achieved with strong, pungent, and sharp-tasting elements that would be overpowering and even unpleasant if eaten on their own. Only when placed with their opposite taste and blended are these strong tastes not only tamed, but also perfumed with aromas of the exotic. The intense fiery heat of spices, pepper, and chilli can be countered with something sweet or neutral. This can be in the form of yoghurt or coconut cream, fruits, sugars, honey, roasted root vegetables, or young baby greens, to name but a few. Strong-tasting salty elements such as fish sauce, soy sauce, and other fermented pastes are harnessed by sour citrus, lemongrass, lime leaves, or tamarind. Together the elements of hot, sweet, salty, and sour become much more than the sum of their parts. This simple rule of thumb helps to ensure that all the food is deliciously vibrant and addictive. Whenever I am travelling in Asia, I sample so many different dishes of enormous variety, yet you can always trace this simple balance of taste and flavour running through them.

The Vietnamese dipping sauce *nuoc cham*, for example, is made by first crushing garlic and salt using a stone mortar and pestle, then adding chopped hot fresh red chilli and pounding together to make a paste. Fresh lime juice and fish sauce are combined and mixed with the paste with a little sugar. The result is mind-blowingly good and very simple and effective. In Thailand, *nam pla prik* is the simplest condiment present on every table – it is simply fish sauce and chopped hot red chilli. When these hot, sour, and salty dressings are placed alongside something sweet such as grilled prawns, fresh crab, or some roasted chicken or pork, the result is astounding because all your taste buds are stimulated at once. You taste all the elements separately, then together.

Whether preparing a simple sauce or a complex meal, the Asian cook weaves a magic web of taste combinations. These can be hearty and comforting in the first mouthful; delicate and exotic in the next. The food of Asia stimulates all the senses.

The recipes that I have researched in my travels and experiences in Asia are to be enjoyed together. In an authentic Asian meal, numerous courses come to the table in a continual stream, and any number of dishes are eaten together. Unlike as in Western cuisines, there is no real separation of dishes or courses. A soup may be eaten alongside a curry or relish, and used to moisten the rice accompanying the meal. The recipes that follow work well when they are served in combination. The book's title, *Asian Bites*, signifies small bite-sized pieces that can be tasted on their own or as part of a larger selection. Different mouthfuls can be sampled as snacks, light meals, or sumptuous feasts that illustrate a broader eating experience of Asia.

Smoking hot

Charcoal braziers, smoky grills and barbecues, the
sizzle of a hot wok – all bring to mind fast food but
good food. Whether it is spicy grilled fish, skewers
of marinated meat, or an exotic vegetable stir-fry,
you will find something to tempt you here. Grilling
and barbecuing are something of an art form in
many parts of Asia, where cooking outside is often
the norm and all manner of street food is available.
And, of course, there is the fine art of stir-frying – a
way to bring fresh, crisp vegetables and succulent
meat or seafood to the table in a tasty flash.

Patta kaah ju chatni | Seared scallops with fresh chutney

The flavours and textures of the vivid green fresh chutney here combine with sweet seared scallops and roasted nuts to make the layered dimensions of this simple dish complete. You could use peanuts or coconut instead of cashews. Different herbs can also be used, while lemon juice or tamarind pulp could provide the sourness.

Serves 6

For the chutney

4 tablespoons raw cashew nuts

1 garlic clove

½ teaspoon salt

1 teaspoon sugar

4 medium-hot fresh green chillies, deseeded and finely chopped

1 large bunch of fresh coriander, stems and leaves roughly chopped

1 tablespoon Greek-style yoghurt

juice of 2 limes

For the scallops

12–18 queen scallops

12–18 scallop shells, cleaned

4cm (1¾in) piece of fresh root ginger

2 tablespoons vegetable oil

3 spring onions, finely sliced

small handful of fresh coriander or mint leaves, roughly chopped

salt and freshly ground black pepper

Partner with
Curried sweetcorn fritters (pp70–1)
Fresh lettuce cups with chicken (pp124–5)

1 To make the chutney, dry-roast the cashew nuts until golden brown; set aside half of the nuts to garnish the scallops. Blend or process the remaining cooled nuts to a paste with the garlic, salt, and sugar. Add the chilli and coriander, and purée. Lastly, add the yoghurt and 2 tablespoons water, and bring together. Purée until smooth or with a bit of texture remaining. You can alter the texture to suit your taste. Transfer the fresh chutney to a bowl, and add the lime juice. Check the seasoning. It should be hot from the chilli; sweet from the nuts and yoghurt; and salty and sour from the lime juice.

2 Clean the scallops by removing the small opaque muscle from the side, which attaches the scallop meat to the shell. The orange-coloured roe can be left on, depending on your taste. Dry the scallops on layers of kitchen paper. Meanwhile, finely slice the ginger, then restack the slices and finely shred into a thin needles. Lightly crush the reserved cashew nuts.

3 Heat the oil in a large heavy sauté pan over a medium-high heat. Season the scallops with salt and black pepper. Add to the pan. Sear for 60–80 seconds on each side, depending on their thickness. To turn the scallops quickly, use two dessertspoons, one in each hand; flick the scallops over from one spoon to the other. When the scallops are caramelized, remove and place on clean kitchen paper.

4 Place a scallop in each shell. Spoon over a little of the green cashew chutney, sprinkle with some shredded ginger and spring onion, followed by some crushed cashew nuts and some fresh herbs. Serve immediately. The chutney is very versatile, and goes well with other seafood dishes such as fresh crab, grilled prawns or lobster, or skewers of firm white fish.

Rau xanh toi xao | Stir-fried greens with garlic

Like much of Vietnamese food, this dish is incredibly simple and delicious. When cooking in a wok, you get an excellent smoky taste to the greens. I had this in Hanoi with pumpkin stems, the green curly vines that attach to the pumpkin from the main plant. It was completely amazing. Try to get hold of pumpkin stems if you can, as they are so tasty. I recommend that either you start growing some yourself or look for them in continental grocers such as Italian, Spanish, or Greek greengrocers, where they are often sold. If not available, use any other greens.

1 If using pumpkin stems, peel the stringy outside fibres as you would celery, and cut into 8cm (3in) lengths. If using other greens, cut into equal-sized pieces. Boil a pan of lightly salted water. Blanch the greens and courgette for 3 minutes or until they still have some bite. Strain the vegetables.

2 Heat the oil in a wok or pan until hot. Add the garlic and stir-fry for 1–2 minutes until golden. Add the blanched greens and courgette, and stir-fry for just long enough to coat in the oil and garlic. Season with salt and lots of black pepper. Add the fish sauce and lemon juice, and stir-fry for a further 30 seconds. Serve immediately as part of a meal with meat, fish, or rice.

Serves 4

1kg (2¼lb) raw pumpkin stems or spinach, silver beet, chard, asparagus, purple sprouting broccoli, or broccoli florets

3 baby courgettes, thinly sliced lengthways

a little vegetable oil for stir-frying

3 small garlic cloves, crushed

2 tablespoons fish sauce such as nuoc nam

juice of 1 lemon

salt and freshly ground black pepper

Partner with
Indonesian fried rice (p32)
Spring onion pancakes (pp60–1)
Malay beef rendang (pp148–9)

Mee goreng | Malaysian fried noodles

The spicy chilli paste for these delicious noodles can be made in a larger batch that, once cooked, can kept in the refrigerator and used when required – a little of this paste goes quite a long way, depending on your chilli tolerance. You could make the noodles themselves as a vegetarian dish by increasing the amount of vegetables and tofu; however, it is more typical to have a combination of chicken, tofu, and prawns.

Serves 4

10 large dried chillies

5 shallots, peeled

5 garlic cloves, peeled

1 teaspoon balachan (shrimp paste)

6 tablespoons vegetable oil

150g (5oz) firm silken tofu, cut into 2cm (1in) cubes

2 onions, chopped

2 garlic cloves, finely chopped

300g (10oz) skinless chicken breast, cut into slices

300g (10oz) raw prawns, peeled and deveined

6 choi sum, Chinese flowering cabbage, or bok choy stems, cut into 3cm (1¼in) lengths

1 teaspoon tomato purée

1 tablespoon dark soy sauce

500g (1lb 2oz) fresh thin yellow wheat noodles (*mee*), cut into short pieces

4 spring onions, finely chopped

200g (7oz) beansprouts, trimmed and rinsed

juice of ½–1 lime

salt and freshly ground black pepper

lime wedges, to serve

1 To make the chilli paste, soak the large dried chillies in boiling water for 20 minutes until softened. Deseed and finely chop. Using a mortar and pestle, pound with the shallot and garlic into a paste. Add the balachan and 2 tablespoons water, and work together. Heat 1 tablespoon of the vegetable oil in wok over a medium-high heat, and fry the paste for 3–4 minutes, transfer to a bowl and wipe out the wok.

2 Heat the remaining oil until hot, and fry the tofu for 3–4 minutes until golden brown. Remove from the wok with a slotted spoon, and drain on kitchen paper. Add the onion and garlic to the oil, and stir-fry for 2 minutes until fragrant. Add the chicken and stir-fry for a further 2–3 minutes. Next, add the prawns and cabbage.

3 Add 1 tablespoon of the chilli paste, the tomato purée, 125ml (4fl oz) water, and the soy sauce, and bring to a simmer. Add the *mee* noodles (which are available at Asian grocers and Chinese supermarkets), and stir-fry for 3 minutes. Lastly, add the spring onion and beansprouts, and return the tofu to the wok. Mix together. Taste, then adjust the flavouring with salt and black pepper, and a little lime juice. The prawns, chicken, and noodles will be sweet; the chilli paste will be hot; the soy sauce and the seasoning will be salty; and the lime juice will be sour. Serve immediately with lime wedges.

Suk ju | Stir-fried bean sprouts with hot red bean paste

Quick to make and very tasty, *suk ju* is one of the many vegetarian dishes that are present on every table in Korea. These dishes are collectively referred to as *namul* and go towards making a fully balanced Korean feast. Kochujang, or hot red bean paste, gains its fire factor from chillies, adding to the spiciness of this dish.

1 Heat the wok or pan over a medium-high heat – it must be hot before you start to cook. Heat the oil, add the garlic, and stir-fry for 30 seconds until fragrant. Add the beansprouts, sesame oil, light soy sauce, and kochujang. Cook quickly for 1–2 minutes until the beansprouts start to wilt.

2 Once the beansprouts have wilted slightly, season well with salt and black pepper. Add the lime juice and coriander leaves. Toss together and taste. The dish will be hot, sweet, salty, and sour; the bean sprouts should still have a lot of bite and not be soggy.

3 Serve straight away, as the sprouts will continue to cook from the residual heat – although they are also delicious cold. In the latter case, a little extra softening doesn't matter, as long as you allow the sprouts to cool as quickly as possible by removing them from the wok as soon as they are cooked.

Serves 4–6 as a side dish

1 tablespoon vegetable oil

2 garlic cloves, finely chopped

750g (1lb 10oz) beansprouts, picked and rinsed

1 tablespoon sesame oil

1 tablespoon light soy sauce

2 teaspoons Sanchung kochujang (Korean hot red bean paste)

juice of 1 lime

handful of fresh coriander, leaves picked

salt and freshly ground black pepper

Partner with
Pork and cabbage dumplings (p75)
Fried squid flowers with ginger and spices (pp58–9)

Ikan panggang | Marinated grilled mackerel

Fresh mackerel is a delicious and simple fish when cooked quickly on a hot grill. In this recipe it is sliced into thick steaks before cooking, but you can also leave the fish whole for grilling – and serving – if you prefer. Mackerel is easy to prepare and cook because of its size. The fantastic marinade here features some of the key ingredients of Indonesian cooking that make the food of this region so distinctive. Turmeric, ginger, lemongrass, and lime are combined with coconut cream to make the hot and sour marinade. The heat and sourness cut the fattiness of the mackerel, working to bring out the sweetness of the fish.

Serves 4–6

2 limes, plus extra lime wedges, to serve

5 fresh red chillies, deseeded and finely chopped

1 teaspoon salt

2 lemongrass stalks, tough outer layer removed, finely chopped

4cm (1¾in) piece of fresh root ginger, finely chopped

5 shallots, finely chopped

200ml (7fl oz) coconut cream

1 teaspoon ground turmeric

4–6 whole mackerel, cleaned and cut into thick steaks

1 Cut the skin and pith from the limes with a sharp knife, exposing the flesh. Discard the rind and pith; finely chop the flesh.

2 Using a mortar and pestle, start grinding the chilli and salt. Add the lemongrass and ginger, and work into a paste. Next, add the softer ingredients – first the shallots, then the diced lime flesh. Add some of the coconut cream to bring the paste together. Transfer the marinade to a wide bowl with the remaining coconut cream. Sprinkle in the ground turmeric and mix together.

3 If you are cooking the mackerel whole, you will need to cut 3 diagonal slits through the skin and down to the bone on both sides of the fish first, to allow the marinade to penetrate right into the centre. Otherwise, simply add the fish steaks to the marinade as they are. Leave to marinate for 30 minutes, spreading the paste over the fish several times while it is doing so.

4 Heat a barbecue or ridged cast-iron grill pan until hot. Grill the fish for 4–5 minutes on each side until browned and cooked through, basting frequently with the spice marinade. Serve straight away with the extra lime wedges for squeezing over, as a snack or starter, or as part of a larger Asian meal.

Partner with
Burmese spiced split pea fritters (pp90–1)
Hot and sour green papaya salad (pp144–5)

Paigu | Chinese barbecue spare ribs

These are easy to make and very tasty. Make sure that you buy plenty of ribs because your guests will find it difficult to stop eating them once they have started. Make these ribs as hot and spicy as you want.

1 Ask your butcher to cut the spare ribs crosswise into thirds that measure 4–5cm (1¾–2in) in length. Put the spare ribs in a large pan of water and bring to the boil. Reduce the heat, and simmer for 20 minutes. Drain and allow to cool. Cut the ribs between the bones to separate them.

2 Mix together all the remaining ingredients except the salt and black pepper in a large bowl. Add the separated spare ribs, and toss together to coat in the marinade. Cover and leave to marinate in the refrigerator for 3–5 hours, or overnight if possible.

3 When you are ready to cook, line a baking tray with foil and heat the oven to 180°C (350°F/Gas 4). Spread out the ribs on the tray, and pour over the marinade. Season well with salt and black pepper. Bake in the oven for 45 minutes, turning once during cooking, until the ribs are golden to dark brown. Serve with lots of paper napkins for wiping sticky fingers.

Serves 4–6

1.5kg (3lb 3oz) Chinese-style pork spare ribs

125ml (4fl oz) hoisin sauce

3 tablespoons light soy sauce

3 tablespoons Shaoxing rice wine

1 tablespoon soft brown sugar

1 tablespoon honey

2 tablespoons tomato purée

4 garlic cloves, finely chopped

3 x 5cm (2in) pieces of fresh root ginger, finely chopped

2 fresh red chillies, deseeded and finely chopped

salt and freshly ground black pepper

Partner with
Prawn and chive spring rolls (pp72–3)
Mushroom pot-sticker dumplings (pp106–7)

Cha bo | Grilled beef patties with shallots and cumin

In Vietnam, these great, well-flavoured beef patties are grilled on bamboo skewers over sizzling charcoal braziers. They are often served as part of a festive meal called *bo bay mon*, where seven different courses of beef are served at one sitting.

Serves 4

For the beef patties

3 tablespoons sesame seeds

1 teaspoon ground cumin

500g (1lb 2oz) lean beef mince

1 garlic clove, very finely chopped

4 shallots, finely chopped

1 tablespoon fish sauce such as nuoc nam

2 tablespoons coconut cream

½ teaspoon curry powder

½ teaspoon sugar

½ teaspoon salt

freshly ground black pepper

For the dipping sauce

3 small fresh bird's-eye chillies, deseeded and thinly sliced

1 garlic clove, finely chopped

1 tablespoon sugar

100ml (3½fl oz) warm water

juice of 2 limes

4 tablespoons fish sauce such as nuoc nam

1 Soak 8 bamboo skewers in cold water for at least 30 minutes, to prevent them burning. Toast the sesame seeds in a dry frying pan over a medium-high heat for about a minute until golden brown. Add the cumin and cook for a further minute until fragrant. Mix all the ingredients for the beef patties together, and leave to rest in the refrigerator for 20–30 minutes.

2 To make the *nuoc cham* dipping sauce, using a mortar and pestle, crush two-thirds of the chilli with the garlic and sugar until smooth. Add the warm water, then transfer to a bowl and add the lime juice and fish sauce. Stir to dissolve the sugar. Set aside.

3 Heat a ridged cast-iron grill pan or char-grill until hot. Divide the beef mixture into 16 portions. Shape each portion into a ball, then gently flatten in your palms to form a 4cm (1½in) patty. Thread two patties onto each bamboo skewer. Grill the beef patties in the pan or over the hot grill for 3 minutes on each side. It is important that you do not overcook them, as this will dry them out – the beef should be medium-rare in the middle. Quickly sprinkle the remaining chilli into the *nuoc cham* dipping sauce (which is hot, salty, and sour), and serve at the table alongside the beef patties for dipping.

Partner with
Spicy green beans with chilli (pp30–1)
Isaan-style grilled chicken (pp40–1)

Keynotes | **Ginger**

This tropical rhizome has been used in many forms across Asia for centuries. Ginger (*Zingiber officinale*) has extraordinary culinary and medicinal value, and it is said to be impossible to cook Asian food without it. Every part of the ginger stem can be utilized, imparting an exhilarating spiciness to salads or seafood dishes. The flesh can be pounded, and the juice squeezed from the pulp to be added to dressings and soups. The remaining pulp then becomes a staple ingredient in countless curry pastes, or provides the base of cooked dishes. The skin is used to flavour stocks, broths, braises, and poaching liquids. Ginger can also be used to cut richness, as seen when it is paired with, for example, coconut cream, pork, or roasted duck.

Ginger

Galangal

Turmeric

Balancing flavours

Ginger plays an essential role in the balance of Asian cooking. It can be part of a larger group of flavours with other herbs and spices, or take more of a lead role in the flavour of a dish. When eaten on its own, ginger is hot and peppery, and you would think too overpowering to go with milder elements, but when blended with other ingredients its chameleon-like properties come to the fore. It partners well with chilli, with garlic, and with the sour elements of lemon, lemongrass, lime juice, and lime leaves favoured in Southeast Asia. The pink-tinged flesh

"Ginger plays an essential role in the balance of Asian cooking. It can be part of a larger group of flavours with other herbs and spices, or take more of a lead role in the flavour profile of a dish."

of young ginger is delicious pickled in rice vinegar; known as *gari* in Japan, it is served alongside every portion of sushi the world over. This "baby" ginger is served in syrup in China, and crystallized for use in confectionery and desserts. Young green ginger flowers are delicious at the beginning of the season. They can be stir-fried, imparting their ginger essence and the crisp texture of asparagus. A wild ginger, or *gra chai*, is used in salads, and marinades for curing fish. It has a milder, earthier taste and wetter texture.

Good medicine

Across Asia, ginger is widely used for its medicinal qualities as an antioxidant, its ability to boost the immune system to fight colds and headaches, and to aid digestion. It helps to combat nausea and is also said to counter many of the bacteria that cause sickness when meat and fish are past their

best. In tropical Asian climates, this can happen very quickly. In the holistic approaches of ayurvedic and traditional Chinese medicine, in particular, ginger has an important role because of its carminative and digestive properties, among other things.

Galangal

Cousins of the ginger rhizome are also important in Asian cooking. One of these is galangal (*Alpinia* spp.), which has a much more fiery, indeed almost medicinal taste than its counterpart. Galangal is largely used in Thailand and Indonesia as a key ingredient in many curry pastes. It is also often found in slices in soups such as *tom yam*, which translates as "hot and sour". It was not until after the Spanish and Portuguese brought back examples of South America's bountiful natural larder that chillies found their way into Thailand in the late 16th century. For centuries previous, ginger and galangal provided the heat and spiciness that form the basis of Thai cooking.

Turmeric

Bright orange turmeric (*Curcuma domestica*) is used fresh in Southeast Asian and South Indian cooking. It has a clean spicy taste similar to ginger and is highly valued for medicinal uses from China across Southeast Asia to India. It has even found champions in Western circles for its anti-cancer properties. In Bali, turmeric is the main ingredient of *jarmu*, a liquid herbal base of medicines used throughout this region. Turmeric is also famed for its dyeing properties – everything that it touches turns a bright yellow.

Kacang panjang | Spicy green beans with chilli

This is a simple and very tasty dish that is a standard item on Chinese and Malay hawker stalls throughout Singapore. Traditionally yard-long beans are used; these are also called snake beans. They have a slightly tougher texture and more flavour than regular green beans; however, they are likely to be found only in Chinese and Asian food stores, or specialty greengrocers. If you have trouble finding them, green beans, mangetout, or asparagus can be used instead.

Serves 4

4 tablespoons vegetable oil

400g (14oz) yard-long beans, chopped into 4cm (1¾in) lengths, or a combination of green beans and asparagus, trimmed and halved

1 tablespoon fish sauce such as nam pla

1 teaspoon sugar

For the spice paste

1 lemongrass stalk, tough outer layer removed, finely chopped

3 slices of fresh root ginger, chopped

5 garlic cloves, finely chopped

3 fresh red chillies, deseeded and finely chopped

10 shallots, chopped

1 tablespoon balachan (shrimp paste)

8 macadamia nuts, roughly chopped

1 To make the spice paste, use a mortar and pestle to pound the ginger and lemongrass to a paste. Add the garlic and chilli, and continue to work. Finally, add the shallot, balachan, and macadamia nuts, and keep working until you have a smooth spice paste.

2 Heat the oil in a wok over a medium-high heat, and fry the spice paste for 4–5 minutes until thick and fragrant. Add the beans, fish sauce, and sugar, and stir-fry for another 4–5 minutes until tender but still with a bite. While you are stir-frying the beans, splash with a little water to create steam. Use only what you need – about 100ml 3½fl oz in all should do. At the end, the beans should be cooked, but not swimming in liquid. Serve immediately.

Partner with
Singapore coconut
laksa (p112)
Roast pork with fresh mint and
peanuts (pp158–9)

Nasi goreng | Indonesian fried rice

One of Indonesia's most famous dishes, *nasi goreng* is available in variation throughout this massive archipelago of islands. It is prepared in countless ways, depending on the availability of ingredients or the chef's inclinations. If you have been put off by a bad example, please try this tempting version. Make it plain to accompany fish or meat dishes, eggs, or sate, or alternatively add pieces of chicken or pork, seasonal vegetables, or prawns and seafood.

Serves 4–6

250g (9oz) mixed fresh mushrooms such as shiitake, field mushrooms, and oyster mushrooms, chopped

2 garlic cloves, finely chopped

5cm (2in) piece of fresh root ginger, peeled and finely chopped

2 fresh red chillies, deseeded and finely chopped

5 shallots, finely chopped

2 tablespoons vegetable oil

500g (1lb 2oz) cold cooked rice such as basmati or jasmine

1 egg, lightly beaten

1 tablespoon ketjap manis (available from Southeast Asian grocers and Chinese supermarkets)

1 tablespoon light soy sauce

1 bunch of fresh asparagus, cut into 3cm (1¼in) lengths

handful of mangetout, topped and tailed (optional)

4 spring onions, finely chopped

1 small bunch of fresh coriander, leaves picked

2 limes

salt and freshly ground black pepper

1 Preheat the oven to 200°C (400°F/Gas 6). Toss the mushrooms with the garlic, ginger, chilli, shallot, and a little of the oil. Season with salt and black pepper. Spread the mixture out on a baking tray, and bake in the oven for 10 minutes until the mushroom and shallot have started to caramelize.

2 Break up the rice with a fork so that the grains are separated. (It is best to use cold leftover rice. If the rice is warm, it absorbs too much oil. If cooking rice just for this dish, cool it as quickly as possible; rice that is kept warm for a long time is prone to dangerous bacteria.) Lightly grease a non-stick frying or omelette pan with a couple of drops of oil. Fry the beaten egg to make a light omelette, allow to to cool, then roll up and cut into thin shreds. Set aside.

3 Heat a wok over a high heat. Add the remaining oil and baked mushroom mixture – make sure you get any juices from the bottom of the pan. Add the rice, ketjap manis, and light soy sauce, and stir-fry for 2 minutes. Add the asparagus and mangetout, if using. Stir constantly for 4–5 minutes until the rice is heated all the way through and the green vegetables are cooked, but still have a bite.

4 Add the spring onion, coriander, and shredded omelette. Add the juice of ½ lime, leaving the rest of the lime to garnish each dish. Check the seasoning. It should be sweet, rich, and earthy; hot from the chilli; and salty from the soy sauce. The lime juice adds a much-needed edge to the richness of the dish. Serve with the remaining lime cut into wedges for squeezing over.

Phat neua | Stir-fried beef with chilli and onion relish

The method of stir-frying was brought to Thailand by the Chinese. Unlike a Chinese stir-fry, which traditionally has soy sauce as a condiment, a Thai stir-fry is served with the fiery *nam pla prik* (chopped bird's-eye chillies with fish sauce and a little sugar). You will see this throughout Thailand on every table at any street food stall or café.

1 Heat the wok over a high heat and add the oil – it will be smoky, so act quickly. Stir-fry a third of the meat, spread out around the wok, for 2–3 minutes until browned. Remove from the pan and set aside. Repeat with the rest of the beef, cooking in three batches in all. Return all the beef to the pan, and reduce the heat to medium.

2 Add the chilli and onion relish and the asparagus. Simmer for 2 minutes, then add the spring onion. Cook for a minute or so until the vegetables are tender, but still crisp. Add the chilli and beansprouts; stir-fry very briefly. Toss through the coriander and mint leaves. Sprinkle over the lime juice. Check the seasoning. Serve with rice or noodles as a simple meal, or as a part of a larger selection.

Nam prik pow (chilli and onion relish) Preheat the oven to 200°C (400°F/Gas 6). In a bowl, mix together 4 roughly chopped onions, 4 chopped garlic cloves, 6 deseeded and finely chopped fresh red chillies and 1½ tablespoons vegetable oil. Spread the mixture out on a baking tray, then roast in the oven for 15–20 minutes until soft and caramelized. Scrape the contents of the tray into a food processor or blender. Add 2 tablespoons soft brown sugar and 1 teaspoon salt; blend to a paste. Add 2 tablespoons tamarind pulp, 2 tablespoons fish sauce (nam pla), and 100ml (3½fl oz) water; blend to a smooth pulp. Heat 1½ tablespoons oil in a heavy pan over a medium-high heat. Add the chilli and onion pulp, reduce the heat and cook for 20–30 minutes until the excess liquid has cooked away. Add the juice of 1 lime, and mix together. Check the seasoning. Pour into sterilized jars and seal with tight-fitting lids. The relish will keep for about a month in the refrigerator. You can make a large batch, and use it to transform anything from a stir-fry to a roast beef sandwich.

Serves 4

2 tablespoons vegetable oil

500g (1lb 2 oz) tender beef, cut into thin strips for stir-frying

3 tablespoons chilli and onion relish (see recipe below)

150g (5oz) trimmed asparagus, cut into 3cm (1¼in) lengths

4 spring onions, finely sliced on the diagonal

1 large fresh medium-hot chilli, deseeded and finely chopped

handful of beansprouts, rinsed and trimmed

handful of fresh coriander leaves

20 fresh mint leaves

juice of 1 lime

steamed rice or noodles, to serve

Partner with
North Vietnamese fish brochettes (pp46–7)
Pickled daikon salad with fried garlic (p142)

Chao tom | Spiced prawn cakes on sticks of lemongrass

Chao tom is a spiced prawn pâté that can be grilled or fried, or wrapped in a banana leaf and steamed. This recipe is traditionally made by making "lollipops" of the paste around one end of sticks of sugar cane, then grilled. The sugar cane caramelizes and imparts a rich essence to the prawn cakes. Fresh sugar cane is quite difficult to get your hands on; lemongrass is more readily available. Use halved lemongrass stalks as the sticks of these prawn lollipops. When heated, the lemongrass imparts its unique perfume right into the centre of the prawn cakes.

Serves 6

12 lemongrass stalks

1kg (2¼lb) large raw tiger prawns, peeled and deveined

2 garlic cloves, finely chopped

3cm (1¼in) piece of fresh root ginger, finely chopped

2 fresh green chillies, deseeded and finely chopped

1 egg white

1 tablespoon fish sauce such as nuoc nam

juice of 1 lime

1 tablespoon rice flour

salt and freshly ground black pepper

1 Trim the root end of the lemongrass, but leave the core, which will hold the stalk together. Cut the stems so that they are about 10–12cm (4–5in) long. (The remaining pieces can be used for another dish.) Remove the tough outer layer of the trimmed stalks, and cut the stalks in half through the core so that you have 24 half-stems, held in place by the core. Set aside.

2 Put the prawns, garlic, ginger, and chilli into a food processor. Season well with salt and black pepper. Add the remaining ingredients, and blend to combine into a paste. Do not overwork – otherwise the mixture will become tough. Fry a small piece of the mixture so that you can taste and adjust the seasoning accordingly. Vietnamese dipping sauces for this sort of snack are often salty and sour; the prawn meat will be quite sweet.

3 Preheat a ridged cast-iron grill pan or barbecue. Roll the prawn mixture into 24 balls, and press a prepared lemongrass stem into each one. Mould the pâté around the stem like a lollipop. Grill the prawn cakes for about 2 minutes on each side, and serve hot with a Vietnamese dipping sauce such as the *nuoc cham* on p38.

Partner with
Sumatran aubergine sambal (pp88–9)
Spring onion and chive flower rolls (pp110–11)

Nem nuong | Minced pork balls with garlic and pepper

In Vietnam, where I first had these pork balls, they are cooked over sizzling braziers on street corners when it starts to get dark. The hot coals are fanned so that they glow and crackle. There is a throng of people returning home after work, and the stalls do a roaring trade. You can buy a single skewer, then some extra highly flavoured pork balls, which are given to you in a small plastic bag that you can delve into as you are bustled along by the crowd.

Serves 6

2 tablespoons raw skinless peanuts

500g (1lb 2oz) lean pork mince

½ teaspoon salt

200g (7oz) hard pork fatback (available from your butcher)

1 teaspoon sugar

2 garlic cloves, finely chopped

2 fresh red chillies, deseeded and finely chopped

1 tablespoon fish sauce such as nuoc nam

1 tablespoon crushed black peppercorns

small handful of fresh coriander leaves, roughly chopped

Nuoc cham dipping sauce

1 teaspoon rice vinegar

1 teaspoon sugar

1 fresh red chilli, deseeded and finely chopped

1 garlic clove, finely chopped

juice of 1 lime

2 tablespoons fish sauce such as nuoc nam

1 Soak 12 bamboo skewers in cold water for at least 30 minutes to prevent scorching. To make the dipping sauce, bring 60ml (2fl oz) water to the boil with the rice vinegar and sugar, then allow to cool. Mix in the chilli, garlic, and lime juice, then stir in the fish sauce. Set aside. Dry-roast the peanuts in a heavy pan over a medium-high heat for 3–4 minutes until golden brown. Remove from the pan. When the nuts are cool, roughly crush. Also set aside.

2 Mix the pork mince with the salt and set aside. Fry the pork fatback in a heavy pan over a medium-high heat for about 10 minutes until partially crisp. Cut into very thin strips, then cut the strips into small dice. The fat adds a great deal of flavour and keeps the mixture moist. Marinate the strips in the sugar, garlic, chilli, fish sauce, and crushed black peppercorns for 5 minutes.

3 Combine the two pork meats, including the marinade, and add the coriander. Make a small ball of the mixture, and cook so that you can taste the ingredients. It should be sweet from the sugar and the fat, hot from the chilli and the pepper, and salty from the fish sauce and the salt. Adjust the seasoning accordingly. Remember that the dipping sauce will be salty, hot, and sour.

4 Heat a char-grill or barbecue until very hot. Roll the mixture into small balls, and thread them onto the skewers, allowing three or four per skewer. Grill evenly on both sides for 4–5 minutes until a mid brown and cooked all the way through. Scatter the skewers with the crushed peanuts, and serve with the *nuac cham* dipping sauce.

Kai yaang | Isaan-style grilled chicken

The Isaan region in the northeast of Thailand close to Laos has a cuisine that is famous for its clean flavours and use of herbs. *Kai yaang* uses a delicious method of rubbing a paste into the meat and marinating it, then grilling it very slowly so that the flavours caramelize on the skin. This is often done with half a chicken that is flattened out and grilled, then cleaved into pieces. The method here is a bit more manageable.

1 Using a mortar and pestle, grind the lemongrass with the salt and sugar to make a rough paste. Add the garlic and coriander root or stems; continue to pound. Next, add the crushed black pepper, and pound until you have a semi-smooth paste. Finally, add the fish sauce and mix until well blended. Rub the chicken thoroughly with the paste, and marinate in the refrigerator for at least 2 hours.

2 Preheat a ridged cast-iron grill pan or charcoal barbecue until hot, but not too hot. The chicken is cooked slowly to impart a smoky savoury character and allow the marinade to caramelize. Place the chicken in the pan or on the barbecue where it is not too close to the direct heat. Turn frequently – every 3 minutes or so – to prevent burning. When the chicken has caramelized on the outside and the meat is cooked, serve with the Isaan dipping sauce below.

Nam jaew (Isaan dipping sauce) Using a pair of scissors, cut the tops off 3 large dried chillies, and split the chillies up the middle. Deseed. Put the chillies in a bowl, and cover with boiling water. Leave for 30 minutes until softened. Wrap 2 teaspoons kapi (Thai shrimp paste) in some foil. Heat a heavy pan over a medium-high heat, and cook the foil parcel for 5 minutes on each side. This makes the paste aromatic, rather than pungent. Chop the drained soaked chilli very finely. Using a mortar and pestle, pound with ½ teaspoon salt and ½ teaspoon sugar to form a rough paste. Add 6 finely chopped shallots and 2 finely chopped garlic cloves; continue to pound. Work in the roasted kapi. Add 2 tablespoons tamarind pulp (see p154), 1 tablespoon fish sauce (nam pla) and 2 tablespoons water. You will be left with a thick jam-like sauce known as a *jaew*.

Serves 4–6

4 lemongrass stalks, tough outer layer removed, finely sliced

1 teaspoon salt

1 teaspoon sugar

6 garlic cloves, finely chopped

3 fresh coriander roots or 6 coriander stems, finely chopped

1 tablespoon crushed black peppercorns

1 tablespoon fish sauce

4 whole chicken breasts, with skin on, each cut into 4 pieces

4 chicken thigh fillets, with skin on, halved

Partner with
Nonya bean curd salad (pp136–7)
Tamarind beef with peanuts (pp180–1)

Keynotes | **Soya products**

It is hard to describe Asian cuisine and culture without mentioning the soya bean and the vast variety of by-products that are produced from this one plant. Soya has been treasured in Asia for

Soya has been treasured in Asia for millennia because of its versatility. In China, soya beans have been grown for about 5,000 years, and their use quickly spread throughout the rest of Asia.

millennia because of its versatility. In China, soya beans have been grown for about 5,000 years, and their use quickly spread throughout the rest of Asia.

Eaten as sprouts and also as young green fresh beans (known as *edamame* in Japan), soya beans are used to produce milk, which can then be turned into tofu or bean curd, which is eaten in China, Japan, and Korea, as well as Thailand and Malaysia. Tempeh, a lightly fermented bean curd, has a nutty flavour. There are many other pastes, sauces, and condiments that use fermented soya beans as a base, and to which other flavours can be added. Then there is soy sauce, both light and dark, used to marinate and infuse, and as an essential condiment in many Asian cultures. In Java, a soy sauce called *ketjap manis* is traditionally sweetened with palm sugar and scented with star anise and galangal.

Soya makes an important nutritional contribution where there is little or no dairy in the diet and meat is scarce and expensive. A single acre of land growing soya beans can yield nearly 20 times more protein than the same acre used for rearing cattle.

Light and dark soy sauce

The use of this quintessential condiment has been documented in Chinese cooking for centuries. It was originally more textured, but today both light and dark soy sauce has been strained of all trace of bean solids. Once used to preserve fresh produce over the winter months, soy sauce is the distilled product of roasted soya beans, flour, and water. These are naturally fermented, then aged.

Light soy sauce is not short on flavour – it is the more salty of the two types. It is good for seafood dishes, vegetables, and light dipping sauces. Dark soy sauce is used much more in Northern China.

Miso

Miso is an essential part of Japanese culture and a cornerstone ingredient in Japanese soups, marinades, spreads, and dressings. It is most commonly used as the base for miso soup – a warm bowl of miso soup is a usual part of a Japanese breakfast. This paste of fermented soya beans varies in colour from pale brown, through red, to dark chocolate brown, depending on whether it is fermented with rice, barley, or wheat. Miso is probably most similar to the original runny Chinese soya bean sauce that was introduced to Japan about 1,000 years ago by Chinese Buddhist monks. Miso has a wine-like pungency and combines brilliantly with ginger, sesame, and Japanese soy sauce, to work as an anchor in the Japanese range of tastes.

Aged for longer than light soy, it contains a dark molasses. Despite its dark colour, it has a softer taste than light soy sauce. Important in the Asian larder, it is suitable for use in stews and braises, and with meat such as duck, beef, and venison.

Tamari

In Japan, use of soy sauce (*shoyu*) can probably be traced back about 1,000 years, when it was introduced by the Chinese. The fermentation method is the same, but Japanese soy sauce tends to have a sweeter, less salty taste, due to a larger proportion of wheat. Tamari is a rich, dark soy sauce made without wheat and much prized in Japan. Unfortunately, not all tamari sold in the West is of the same high quality as in its native Japan.

Tofu and bean curd

Tofu (Japanese) and *doufu* (Chinese name) most likely originated in China during the Han Dynasty (206 BC–AD 220). It is made from yellow soya beans that are soaked, ground, and cooked to form the milk product, which is then solidified and aged. Soft bean curd is called *silken tofu* and often comes packed in water. When the bean curd is deep-fried, the smooth texture transforms into a sponge-like web that is crisp on the outside.

Soya beans

Tofu

Soy sauce

Fermented bean products

Fermented bean curd can be preserved in rice wine, brine, or chillies, to be used in condiments. It can be eaten on its on own or as a condiment, or used in seasoning. Red fermented bean curd is naturally coloured by adding red rice and has a thick consistency. It is often combined with chillies to make a hot bean paste. This is used in Sichuan cooking, as well as in Korea, where it is called *kochujang* and originates from the region of Sunchang. In both these cuisines, it forms an important and distinctive flavouring.

43

Sambal lado mudo | Sardines with green chilli sambal

This is a dish that could be made with fresh sardines, anchovies, or mackerel – all would work well because they are easy to prepare and quick to cook, not to mention very good for you because of the omega-3 oils. You could also serve this sambal with a piece of seared tuna. You need to use unripe green tomatoes; if they are not available, choose the least-ripe tomatoes that you can find, even though this is the opposite of what you usually look for. The hot and sour elements of the sambal cut the oiliness of the fish. Get your fishmonger to clean and scale the fish so that it is even easier to prepare.

1 Peel the shallots and cut in half; remove the core. Finely slice the shallots. Turn the lime leaves over so that the underside is uppermost. Using a sharp knife, shave off the stem so that the leaf lies flat. Place the leaves on top of each other, and tightly roll like a cigar. With a fast rolling motion of the knife, finely chop the lime leaves into a thin needle-like shred.

2 To make up the sambal, heat the 2 tablespoons oil in a heavy pan over a medium-high heat. Add the shallot, and stir-fry for 2 minutes until fragrant and translucent. Add the green chilli, diced tomato, lime leaves, sugar, and salt. Stir-fry for 3 minutes, then add the lime juice and remove the pan from the heat.

3 Heat a frying pan or ridged cast-iron grill pan over a medium-high heat, and add a little oil. Season the fish with salt and black pepper. Grill the fish for 3 minutes on each side. Be careful not to overcook them, as this will cause them to dry out and lose their flavour. Serve immediately with the green chilli and tomato sambal, and enjoy the great combination of tastes.

Serves 4

5 shallots, sliced

2 kaffir lime leaves

2 tablespoons vegetable oil plus extra for cooking

6 green chillies, deseeded and finely chopped

2 unripe green tomatoes, deseeded and flesh diced

2 teaspoons sugar

1 teaspoon salt

juice of 2 limes

12–16 fresh sardines, cleaned and scaled

freshly ground black pepper

Partner with
Nonya-style spicy pork (pp114–15)
Asian salad with pea shoots and sprouts (pp140–1)

Cha ca nuong | North Vietnamese fish brochettes

In Hanoi's old city, the famous Cha Ca Street used to hold a number of restaurants all selling this spectacular marinated fish. The most well known is Cha Ca la Vong, said to be 135 years old and now owned by the sixth generation of the founding family. This recipe is one of the simplified street-food versions sold in the eatery's vicinity.

Serves 4–6

500 g (1 lb 2 oz) firm white fish such as monkfish, snapper, or grouper

1 onion

2 garlic cloves, finely chopped

4cm (1¼in) piece of fresh root ginger, finely chopped

1 fresh red chilli, deseeded and finely chopped

1 teaspoon ground turmeric

5 tablespoons vegetable oil

3 tablespoons fish sauce such as nuoc nam

2 tablespoons Shaoxing rice wine (or mirin or sake)

4 spring onions, finely chopped

½ bunch of fresh dill, picked and chopped

salt and freshly ground black pepper

100g (3½ oz) raw skinless peanuts, dry-roasted until golden, then roughly crushed, to garnish

lime wedges, to serve

1 Clean the fish, removing the bones and the skin (you could ask your fishmonger to do this for you). Cut the flesh into 3cm (1¼ in) cubes, and put into a glass or ceramic dish. Grate the flesh of the onion using a cheese grater, to form a rough pulp. In a bowl, mix the onion, garlic, ginger, and chilli. Add the turmeric, 2 tablespoons of the oil, fish sauce, and rice wine, and stir to combine. Pour the mixture over the cubed fish, and marinate in the refrigerator for 2–3 hours.

2 To make the basting sauce, heat the remaining 3 tablespoons vegetable oil in a pan over a medium-high heat. Add the spring onion and dill. Fry for 2 minutes until fragrant. Remove from the heat and allow to infuse.

3 Soak a handful of short bamboo skewers or wooden cocktail sticks in cold water for at least 30 minutes to avoid scorching. Heat a barbecue or ridged cast-iron grill pan until hot. Skewer the pieces of marinated fish onto the bamboo skewers. Season with salt and black pepper. Grill the brochettes of fish on the hot grill for 2 minutes on each side, basting with the spring onion and dill mixture while grilling. When cooked, scatter with the crushed peanuts, and serve hot with lime wedges.

Partner with
Sichuan chicken
dumplings (p100)
Grilled aubergine salad
(pp128–9)

Char siu | Chinese barbecue pork

In Chinese cuisine the pig, with all its delicious by-products, is revered above all other animals. There are many variations of Chinese barbecue pork; some are more spicy than others, using five-spice in the marinade. It is simple to make and deliciously tasty, and can be used in salads, noodle dishes, soups, and stir-fries. It also features in the Steamed Barbecue Pork Buns on p101.

Serves 4–6

2 garlic cloves

1 teaspoon five-spice powder

3 tablespoons light soy sauce

2 tablespoons red fermented bean curd (available from Chinese supermarkets)

1 tablespoon hoisin sauce

1 tablespoons sugar

3 tablespoons Shaoxing rice wine

600g (1lb 5oz) pork neck or shoulder, cut into strips 3–4cm (1¼–1¾in) thick

2 tablespoons runny honey

1 Crush the garlic and mix with the five-spice powder. Combine with all the remaining ingredients except for the pork and honey. Put the pork in a shallow glass or ceramic dish, and cover with the marinade. Leave to marinate in the refrigerator for at least 4 hours, turning a few times to ensure that the meat is well coated.

2 Heat the oven to 230°C (450°F/Gas 8). Fill a deep baking dish with water, and fit a wire rack over the top. Place the pork directly on the rack. Bake in the oven for 30 minutes, basting the pork with the excess marinade at least three times during the cooking process. Just before the end of the cooking time, heat the overhead grill until very hot.

3 Carefully remove the baking dish from the oven, and brush the pork strips with the honey using a pastry brush or similar. Grill the strips under the overhead grill until the pork caramelizes and chars slightly around the edges. Serve hot with rice, or sliced into stir-fries and soups. Alternatively, you can serve individual portions nestled in Little Gem lettuce leaves, ready to pick up and eat.

Partner with
Steamed green
vegetable rolls (p105)
Nonya pork, prawn, and
crab ball soup (p113)

Naan | Garlic and coriander naan

Naan with garlic is very difficult to resist. This tear-shaped bread originated in the Middle East, but it was the Punjabis who introduced it to the rest of the world. It is traditionally cooked on the sides of a tandoor oven, which produces beautiful puffy results. Naan baked in a conventional oven will be flatter, but still delicious.

1 Whisk the egg, sugar, yoghurt, and milk until smooth. Sift together the flour, pinch of salt, and bicarbonate of soda. Add the yoghurt mixture and combine to make a soft dough. You may need to add a little water, a teaspoon at a time, if the dough seems too stiff. Knead the dough for 3–4 minutes, then add the oil and continue to knead until all the oil has been absorbed into the dough, and the dough is soft and elastic. Put the dough in a bowl, cover with a clean cloth, and leave to rest in a warmish place (room temperature is fine) for 30 minutes.

2 Preheat the oven to 220°C (425°F/Gas 7). Crush the garlic with a little salt to form a paste. Stir the garlic purée into the softened butter with the cayenne pepper, coriander, and spring onion. Season with black pepper, and beat together.

3 Divide the dough into eight balls. Smear a blob of the herb butter onto each dough ball, then flatten the dough so that it is roughly 5mm (¼in) thick and the rough shape of a teardrop. Allow the dough pieces to rise for a further 5 minutes before baking.

4 Lay two pieces on a non-stick baking tray, and bake in the oven for 7 minutes until golden. (If you like, you can have two baking trays going at the same time.) Keep the naan warm while you finish baking the rest. Serve with any combination of Indian, Sri Lankan, and Burmese food.

Makes 8

1 egg
1 teaspoon sugar
1 tablespoon Greek-style yoghurt
125ml (4fl oz) milk
300g (10oz) plain flour
pinch of salt
½ teaspoon bicarbonate of soda
2 tablespoons vegetable oil
4 garlic cloves, finely chopped
50g (1¾oz) softened butter
½ teaspoon cayenne pepper
1 small bunch of fresh coriander, leaves picked
4 spring onions, finely chopped
freshly ground black pepper

Partner with
Sri Lankan smoky aubergine dip (pp150–1)
Lemon and saffron chicken kebabs (pp172–3)

Sate lilit bebek | Sumatran minced duck sate

The West Sumatran region of Padang is famed for its spicy cuisine. The island's wealth of spices such as cinnamon, pepper, chilli, and cumin, as well as turmeric, ginger, galangal, and lemongrass, has been fought over for centuries. These quite unusual sate use minced duck meat or chicken, or a combination of the two.

1 To make the spice paste, use a mortar and pestle to grind the turmeric, coriander seeds, black peppercorns, cloves, and nutmeg into a powder. Add the macadamia nuts. Put the ginger and galangal in a food processor and work to a paste, then add the shallot, chilli, and garlic. Blend together until smooth. Combine the ground spices, palm sugar, and balachan, and add to the food processor with the fresh coriander. Work again to combine. Heat the oil in a saucepan over a medium-high heat. Sauté the spice paste for about 5 minutes until fragrant. Set aside to cool.

2 Meanwhile, prepare the rest of the ingredients. Put the duck meat in the food processor with the salt and crushed black pepper (you do not have to wash the food processor after making the spice paste). Blend into a smooth mince, remove and combine with the chicken and the cooled spice mix. Turn the lime leaves over so that the underside is uppermost. Using a sharp knife, shave off the stem so that the leaf lies flat. Place the leaves on top of each other, and tightly roll like a cigar. With a fast rolling motion of the knife, finely chop the lime leaves into a thin needle-like shred. Combine with the duck mixture and mix together.

3 Remove the tough outer layer of the lemongrass and discard. Cut the stems in half through the middle. Mould 2 tablespoons of the sate mixture tightly around the base end of the lemongrass stem. Grill over a hot barbecue or in a hot ridged cast-iron grill pan for 2–3 minutes on each side until golden brown. Serve immediately. The meat will be perfumed with the spices and fresh lemongrass that have made the island of Padang so famous. You will definitely get the right reaction from your guests when you serve these.

Serves 6

For the spice paste

1.5cm (¾in) piece of dried turmeric or 1½ teaspoons ground turmeric

1 tablespoon coriander seeds

½ teaspoon black peppercorns

2 cloves

pinch of grated nutmeg

8 macadamia nuts

3cm (1¼in) piece of fresh root ginger, finely chopped

3cm (1¼in) piece of galangal, finely chopped (if not available, double the quantity of ginger)

12 shallots, sliced

3 fresh red chillies, deseeded and finely chopped

6 garlic cloves, sliced

2 tablespoons palm sugar

1 teaspoon balachan or kapi (shrimp paste)

handful of fresh coriander leaves

2 tablespoons vegetable oil

500g (1lb 2oz) duck meat

1 teaspoon crushed black peppercorns

1 teaspoon salt

300g (10oz) minced chicken

5 kaffir lime leaves

12–14 lemongrass stems

Bulgogi | Marinated barbecue beef

Bulgogi is an essential part of a Korean meal. Wafer-thin slices of sirloin or topside of beef are steeped in a delicious marinade containing pear and sesame oil. The meat is quickly grilled, then served with a number of different dips, condiments such as *kimch'i*, and vegetable side dishes.

Serves 4

750g (1lb 10oz) aged sirloin or rib eye of beef with a good marbling of internal fat

1 pear

1 onion

3 garlic cloves, finely chopped

pinch of salt

3 tablespoons light soy sauce

2 tablespoons sesame oil

2 teaspoons soft brown sugar

1 tablespoon rice wine such as Shaoxing

freshly ground black pepper

1 Remove any excess fat from the piece of beef, then cut into thin slices. (You could ask your butcher to do this for you.) Peel the pear, and grate the flesh to form a pulp; repeat the same process with the onion. This can then be combined. Using a mortar and pestle, crush the garlic with a pinch of salt to form a paste. Combine the light soy sauce and sesame oil in a bowl. Add the brown sugar and garlic paste, and season with lots of black pepper.

2 Take a handful of the pear and onion pulp, and squeeze the juice into a bowl; discard the pulp. Repeat until you have extracted all the juice. Put the the combined juices, beef, and rice wine in a large bowl. Massage the beef with this acidic liquid for 2 minutes. Pour over the remaining marinade ingredients, cover, and leave to marinate in the refrigerator for 3 hours.

3 Heat a large skillet or ridged cast-iron grill pan over a high heat. Drain the beef slices, and sear in the pan with no oil for 1 minute on each side. Serve with vegetable accompaniments such as spicy *kimch'i*. The beef is sweet, sour, and salty. Serving it with a hot dressing or condiment such as the one accompanying the bream on p143 will mean that you have a balance of all the main tastes.

Partner with
Korean hot pickled cabbage (p164)
Fried aubergine with toasted sesame seeds (p178)

Crisp and fiery

So much of Asian food, from whatever tradition or region it originates, is ideal for communal eating, whether it be a meal around the table with lots of different courses or a casual evening of drinks and canapés. This is not to say that Asian food doesn't also make for great snacks at any time of the day. It does. The problem will be learning to share. The food here ranges from the supremely pick-up-able, such as piping-hot fritters, crisp-battered seafood, and tempting pancakes, to bursts of fire, spice, and heat in sambals, fishcakes, and dumplings.

Vadai | Keralan spiced chickpea and lentil dumplings

Similar in texture to a falafel, these delicious fried dumplings are from Kerala in the south of India. When you are making them, mould them around your little finger like a doughnut. This ensures that, as they are frying the heat gets right into the centre of the fritters, so that the outside becomes crispy, while the inside is light and fluffy.

Serves 6

200g (7oz) urad dal (split black gram)

1 tablespoon vegetable oil plus extra for deep-frying

2 garlic cloves, finely chopped

2 green chillies, deseeded and finely chopped

2 medium onions, finely chopped

10 curry leaves (fresh or dried)

300g (10oz) cooked chickpeas, rinsed and drained

1 small bunch of fresh coriander, leaves picked

100g (3½oz) rice flour

1½ teaspoons garam masala

½ teaspoon curry powder (make your own or buy the freshest Indian blend you can)

½ teaspoon asafoetida powder

½ teaspoon baking powder

salt and freshly ground black pepper

lime or lemon wedges, to serve

Partner with
Rice flour pancakes (p81)
Carrot pachadi (pp162–3)
Potato with turmeric and mustard seeds (pp174–5)

1 Put the urad dal in a bowl, cover with cold water, and soak for 1–1½ hours. Drain, then cover with a fresh batch of cold water. If the dal still has its black husks, plunge your hands into the water, and rub the dal together to remove them – the action is similar to washing your hands. The husks will rise to the surface. Skim off and discard, then drain the dal and again cover with fresh cold water. Continue the rubbing and skimming process for several changes of water, then drain the dal completely. Don't worry about removing all of the husks –just the majority. (If you are using urad dal that has already had the husks removed, simply soak and rinse.)

2 Heat the 1 tablespoon oil in a heavy pan over a medium-high heat. Fry the garlic and green chilli for 2 minutes until fragrant. Add the onion and curry leaves, and continue to fry for 4–5 minutes until softened. Remove from the heat.

3 Put the drained urad dal, chickpeas, onion mixture, and half the fresh coriander in a food processor. Work into a paste until almost smooth, but with a little texture. Transfer to a bowl. Add the rice flour, garam masala, curry powder, asafoetida, baking powder, and remaining coriander, roughly chopped. Mix together, and season with salt and black pepper. Roll the mixture into small balls about 3.5cm (1½in) in diameter; flatten slightly. Make a hole in the centre of each ball with your little finger, so that they are like mini doughnuts.

4 Heat enough oil for deep-frying in a deep-fryer or a large heavy pan over a medium-high heat. Once the oil has reached 180°C (350°F), test with a little of the mixture – it should sizzle and bubble straight away. Fry the dumplings, in small batches, for 2–3 minutes until golden brown. Serve hot with wedges of lemon or lime.

Fried squid flowers with ginger and spices

Squid, prawns, and other sweet seafood lend themselves very well to being fried with a hot and salty coating. It could be salt and pepper, or salt and chilli, or a combination of crushed pepper, dried chilli, and Sichuan pepper. This recipe differs slightly from the usual method of crusting, then frying – it adds another layer of flavours.

Serves 4–6

500g (1lb 2oz) squid

5cm (2in) piece of fresh root ginger, chopped

1 tablespoon Shaoxing rice wine

vegetable oil for deep-frying

2 teaspoons spicy salt and pepper (see below)

fresh coriander leaves, roughly chopped, to garnish

lemon or lime wedges, to garnish

For the spicy salt and pepper

1 tablespoon salt

2 teaspoons ground Sichuan peppercorns

1 teaspoon crushed dried red chilli flakes

1 teaspoon five-spice powder

1 To make the spicy salt and pepper, mix the four ingredients together, and dry-roast in a small frying pan over a medium heat for 2–3 minutes until fragrant. Set aside.

2 Pull out the squid's tentacles, then pull off the side flaps. With a sharp knife, split the tubles open down the natural seam, and scrape off any soft jelly-like substance; discard. Remove the outer skin; discard. Put your thumb and forefinger in front of the ink sac. Push towards the tentacles, exposing the small hard beak. Remove and discard. Cut between the ink sac and tentacles. You will be left with the opened-out tubes and the tentacles. Rinse under cold running water, then pat dry with kitchen paper.

3 Score the inside of the squid with a crisscross pattern, making sure not to slice all the way through. Cut into 3cm x 5cm (1¼in x 2in) pieces. Blanch in a pan of boiling water for 30 seconds. Each piece will curl up, and the crisscross pattern opens out like a flower. Remove with a slotted spoon and refresh in cold water. Remove and once again pat dry with kitchen paper. Using a mortar and pestle, crush the ginger to a pulp. Take the pulp in your hands, and squeeze all the juice into a bowl; discard the pulp. Add the rice wine and squid to the juice, and marinate the squid in the refrigerator for 30 minutes.

4 Fill a wok a quarter full with oil, and heat over a medium-high heat. (To check that the oil is hot enough, fry a piece of bread – it should turn golden in about 15 seconds.) Season the squid with 2 teaspoons spicy salt and pepper. (The rest will keep in a glass jar with a screwtop lid.) Fry the squid for 40 seconds in the hot oil, then remove with a slotted spoon and drain well on kitchen paper. Serve garnished with the coriander and lemon or lime wedges.

Partner with
Sichuan peppered beef (pp170–1)
Fried aubergine with toasted sesame seeds (p178)

Pa jeon | Spring onion pancakes

As with many fine examples of Asian cooking where the ingredients speak for themselves, this Korean stuffed omelette is deliciously simple dish. This version is vegetarian, but traditionally shellfish such as prawns, mussels, or oysters is often added. It works very well with the ginger and sesame dipping sauce.

1 Combine the three flours in a bowl. Whisk in the eggs, then 200ml (7fl oz) water, to make a smooth batter the texture of double cream. Season with the salt and some black pepper. Cut the ginger into thin slices, then restack on your chopping board and finely shred. Add to the batter with the spring onion and chilli (if you are using shellfish, it should be added at this point).

2 Heat a skillet or omelette pan over a medium-high heat. Add a couple of tablespoons of vegetable oil and circulate around the pan, tipping out any excess into a dry cup so that it can be used for the next pancake. Add a small ladleful of the batter to the pan, spreading it out to make a thin pancake about 10cm (4in) in diameter. Cook for about 2 minutes until golden brown on the bottom, then turn over and cook for a further 2 minutes. Repeat the process until all the batter has been used. Serve immediately with the ginger and sesame dipping sauce below.

Ginger and sesame dipping sauce Delicious with *pa jeon*, which usually contains spring onion or oysters, this dipping sauce can be used as a dressing for a salad or as a dipping sauce with fish and shellfish such as raw oysters, grilled prawns, or scallops, or perhaps with some steamed mussels or crab. Using a mortar and pestle, crush 2 peeled garlic cloves with ½ teaspoon dried red chilli flakes, ½ teaspoon salt, and ½ teaspoon sugar until smooth. Transfer to a bowl and add 4 tablespoons light soy sauce, 1 tablespoon rice vinegar, 1 tablespoon sesame oil, and 2 tablespoons vegetable oil. Toast 2 teaspoons sesame seeds in a dry frying pan until golden. While they are still warm, grind to a rough paste using a mortar and pestle; add to the dressing. Check the seasoning.

Serves 4–6

40g (1½oz) glutinous rice flour

40g (1½oz) rice flour

40g (1½oz) plain flour

2 eggs, lightly beaten

1 teaspoon salt

4cm (1¾ in) piece of fresh root ginger

8 spring onions, cut into 3cm (1¼in) lengths

1 fresh red chilli, deseeded and cut into fine slivers

about 2 tablespoons vegetable oil

freshly ground black pepper

1 quantity ginger and sesame dipping sauce (below), to serve

Partner with
Mushroom pot-sticker dumplings (pp106–7)
Cured prawns with shredded lime leaves (p123)

Aloo puri | Fried puffed potato bread

These Indian *puri* are very light and puff up spectacularly, giving everyone the impression that you are a magician in the kitchen. They look much more complicated than they actually are. *Puri* are almost identical to *chapatti*, except that they are deep-fried in hot oil, which is what makes them puff up. The secret to the cooking is to flick hot oil over the surface of the *puri* while the bottom is frying in the oil.

Makes about 30 small puri or 15 large ones

250g (9oz) floury potatoes such as Maris Piper, peeled and cut into equal-sized pieces

2 teaspoons salt

300g (10oz) plain flour

2 tablespoons melted butter

about 100ml (3½fl oz) warm water

vegetable oil for deep-frying

1 Put the potato in a saucepan, and cover with plenty of cold water. Add 1 teaspoon of the salt and bring to the boil. Simmer for 10–12 minutes until tender to the point of a knife. Drain, then return the potato to the pan over a low heat for 2–3 minutes, to allow it to dry out slightly. Mash and allow to cool.

2 Sift the flour and the remaining 1 teaspoon salt into a bowl. Add the mashed potato and stir through. Make a slight well in the centre, and add the melted butter and the water a little at a time, drawing the mixture together until you have a firm dough. Lightly flour your hands and a clean work surface, and knead the dough thoroughly for 10 minutes until soft and elastic. Cover and allow to stand for 30 minutes. (At this stage you could store the dough in the refrigerator for a few hours if well covered, but you get much better "puffy" results if you leave the dough resting for only 30 minutes.)

3 To make either small or large *puri*, roll the dough into 30 small balls (or 15 for the larger ones), then flatten each one into a circle using your hands. Roll out the discs of dough until they are 2–5mm (⅛–¼in) thick. The diameter will vary according to how many you are making.

4 Heat enough oil for deep-frying until very hot. Add one or two *puri* at a time, depending on what size they are – do not crowd the pan. Immediately start to flick oil over the top of the dough so that it starts to puff up. When the *puri* is golden brown on the bottom, flick it over for another moment or two, and cook until golden on this side as well. Drain on kitchen paper. Repeat the process until all the *puri* are cooked. Serve hot with a vegetable curry or similar.

Partner with
Stir-fried beef with chilli and onion relish (p33)
Tomato chutney with green chilli (p179)

Kabak mücveri | Turkish courgette fritters

Istanbul is an extraordinary city filled with contrasts. Standing astride the two continents of Asia and Europe brings ingredients, cuisines, and cultures together to magnificent effect. The use of Mediterranean herbs such as mint and dill, and spices such as cayenne pepper and a little cumin, illustrates just that. The fritters are sweet, salty from the cheese, and hot from the spices. When fried and served with some freshly squeezed lemon juice, they form a perfect combination of flavours.

Serves 4

500g (1lb 2oz) courgettes

2 tablespoons olive oil

1 large onion, finely chopped

1 garlic clove, finely chopped

½ teaspoon cayenne pepper

½ teaspoon ground cumin

3 eggs

3 tablespoons plain flour

30 fresh mint leaves

3 sprigs of fresh dill, leaves picked

200g (7oz) beyaz peynir (white cheese) or feta cheese, broken into small nuggets

a little vegetable oil

salt and freshly ground black pepper

lemon wedges, to serve

1 Cut the courgettes into slices about 1cm (½in) thick. Cut the slices into strips 1cm (½in) wide, then restack the strips and cut the courgette into 1cm (½in) dice.

2 Heat the olive oil in a heavy pan over a medium-high heat. Add the onion, and sweat for 4 minutes until softened. Push the onion to one side to make a little space in the pan. Add the garlic, cayenne pepper, and ground cumin, and sweat for 1–2 minutes until fragrant, then combine with the onion. Add the diced courgette and sauté for 2–3 minutes. Season with salt and black pepper. (The cheese is salty, so be careful not to overseason.) Leave to cool.

3 Beat the eggs in a large bowl, then stir in the flour until you have a smooth batter. Tear the fresh herbs into the batter, and mix in the cheese. Fold in the courgette and onion mixture.

4 Heat enough oil to form a film over the bottom of a frying pan over a medium-high heat. Pour in the batter in half-ladlefuls, to make a few fritters at a time. Cook for about 2 minutes until golden brown, then turn over and cook on the other side for another 2 minutes or so. Drain on kitchen paper, and serve with lemon wedges for squeezing over the top.

Partner with
Spicy lamb-stuffed pancakes (p74)
Spicy apricot chutney (pp160–1)

Rempeyek kacang | Crisp peanut wafers

In Indonesia, these delicious spicy fried wafers contain coconut cream, peanuts, and candle nuts. Candle nuts are commonly used in many Indonesian dishes. They are not that easy to come across, but are similar in taste and texture to the more commonly available macadamia nuts, which make a very good substitute. If these are not available, you could use cashew nuts instead. The crisps can be eaten on their own or as an accompaniment to rice dishes or a vegetable dish such as the famous *gado gado*, a salad of raw and cooked vegetables with a peanut sauce.

1 Spread the peanuts on a roasting tray, and bake in the oven at 180°C (350°F/Gas 4) for 4–5 minutes until pale golden brown. Set aside to cool.

2 To make the spice paste, using a mortar and pestle, work the garlic, coriander seeds, and salt into a paste. Add the candle or macadamia nuts and the shredded lime leaves, and continue to work. Lastly, add the fresh coriander leaves, and season with black pepper. Work until the paste is smooth.

3 Sift the two types of flour and turmeric together in a bowl, then add the coconut cream to make a batter. Add the roasted peanuts, and stir through thoroughly. Taste and season with salt and black pepper if required.

4 Heat a heavy high-sided pan over a medium-high heat, and add the vegetable oil. Test whether the oil is hot enough with a little of the mixture – it should fry and sizzle straight away. Carefully drop a tablespoonful of batter at a time into the hot oil, to form each wafer. Cooking in batches, fry the wafers for 2–3 minutes until they are crisp and golden. Drain on kitchen paper, and serve hot or warm.

Serves 6–8

200g (7oz) skinless raw peanuts
100g (3½oz) plain flour
150g (5oz) rice flour
1 teaspoon ground turmeric
200ml (7fl oz) coconut cream
200ml (7fl oz) vegetable oil for deep-frying
salt and freshly ground black pepper

For the spice paste

2 garlic cloves
1 tablespoon coriander seeds
1 teaspoon salt
2 tablespoons of candle nuts or macadamia nuts
5 kaffir lime leaves, shredded
small handful of fresh coriander leaves

Partner with
Indonesian fried rice (p32)
Crisp cabbage salad with peanuts (pp134–5)

Zard choba pakora | Potato and cauliflower pakoras

Pakoras are delicious and simple street food snacks eaten throughout Northern India, Pakistan, Afghanistan, and Central Asia. These fiery snacks are addictive, and combine spiciness with salt and the sweetness of the vegetables. Accompanied by a wedge of lemon or lime, their balance of flavour is complete.

1 Mix together the coarse-ground coriander seeds, turmeric, cumin, and chilli flakes. Combine the flour and 200ml (7fl oz) water to form a smooth batter. Season with the 2 teaspoons salt and black pepper. Leave to rest for 20 minutes.

2 Meanwhile, scrub the potatoes, put in a pan, and cover well with cold salted water. Bring to the boil, and simmer for 10–12 minutes. Remove from the heat, drain, and allow the potatoes to cool. Blanch the cauliflower in boiling water for 3 minutes until softened slightly, but still with a bite. Drain and allow to cool.

3 Mix the dried spices with the batter and chopped coriander. When the potatoes have cooled, peel off the skin and cut the flesh into 4mm (¼in) slices. Heat the oil for deep-frying in a large heavy pan until hot. Dip the potato slices into the batter, coating well on both sides, then deep-fry them in the hot oil in small batches. (Do not crowd the pan – otherwise the temperature of the oil will drop too much.) The pakoras will rise to the surface once they are cooked. Drain on kitchen paper, and repeat the process with the cauliflower florets. Cook until golden brown. Sprinkle with salt, and serve hot with lemon or lime wedges, or perhaps a coriander or coconut chutney (see pp16 and 133).

Serves 4–6

2 teaspoons coarse-ground coriander seeds

1 teaspoon ground turmeric

½ teaspoon ground cumin

½ teaspoon dried red chilli flakes

175g (6oz) gram flour (Indian chickpea flour)

2 teaspoons salt

4 large potatoes, scrubbed but unpeeled

½ head of cauliflower, broken into even-sized florets

30 fresh coriander leaves, roughly chopped

vegetable oil for deep-frying

freshly ground black pepper

lemon or lime wedges, to serve

Partner with
Turkish courgette fritters (p62)
Indian fresh coconut chutney (p133)

Keynotes | **Curry pastes and spice blends**

The Tamil word *kari*, meaning "sauce", is said to be the origin of the word "curry". It means different things to different people across the vast continent of Asia. Many curries contain chillies, either fresh or dried; however, it was only after the Portuguese had travelled to South America in the 16th century that chillies were introduced to Southeast and South Asia. Before this, black and white pepper were used to create the heat in dishes, along with ingredients such as raw ginger and garlic.

A burgeoning spice trade

Trade in spices has existed between Europe and the east for many centuries. Cooks in the Roman Empire used to grind black pepper, ginger, and cumin that came in on the silk roads from Asia.

"Conquest, religion, trade, and the migration of populations over many centuries have ensured that curries have travelled across Asia and beyond. It is the spices and spice combinations that make each curry from each region so unique."

In the crusades of the 11th century onwards, the European clash with Arab, Persian, and Middle Eastern cultures intensified, and led to a marked increase in the quantity of spices that could be exported. Conquest, religion, trade, and the migration of populations over many centuries have ensured that curries have travelled across Asia and beyond. It is the spices and spice combinations that make each curry from each region so unique.

Spice blends and seasonings

Combinations and special blends of spices are myriad throughout Asia. They are at their best and most fragrant when ground to order from whole spices, then blended. Three particular blends found in Asian cuisine are India's garam masala; five-spice powder, used in China and Vietnam; and Japanese seven-spice, or shichimi togarashi.

India's garam masala is a blend of as many as 15 spices and is used in scores of dishes from curries to chutneys. The word *garam* means "hot", and garam masala is often used instead of chilli. It usually features black pepper, cumin, cardamom, cloves, bay leaves, coriander seeds, cinnamon, nutmeg, and mace. Households and

Shichimi togarashi

spice merchants each have their own special recipes. I highly recommend buying an electric coffee grinder and making your own.

Used in China and Vietnam, five-spice powder has both medicinal and culinary importance. Usually a blend of star anise, cinnamon, cloves, fennel seeds, and Sichuan pepper, its distinctive aroma

Curry leaves

Red
curry
paste

Garam
masala

Green
curry
paste

Thai curry pastes

In Thailand, chopping, grinding, and pounding fresh herbs and spices to form smooth, pungent pastes is the classic basis of curry. These curry pastes are known as *kaeng*. Recipes and categories vary from region to region – sour, hot, dry, forest, mountain, or coastal, as well as yellow and *massaman* (which originated in Persia). Red curry paste, or *kaeng daeng* (red curry) or *kaeng phet* (hot curry), is often used as a spicy base for other curries. Thai green curry paste, or *kaeng kwio waan*, gets its heat from green chillies and can vary in intensity. It is generally more fragrant than red curry paste, using lots of lemongrass, lime leaves, and fresh coriander roots, which are pounded together.

When it comes to cooking, there should be a balance of hot from chilli; sweet from coconut cream and palm sugar; sour from lemongrass, lime leaves, fresh lime juice, and tamarind juice; and salty from fish or soy sauce.

conjures up images of vibrant markets and delicious food.

A delicious Japanese blend of seasonings, shichimi togarashi, or Japanese seven-spice, contains dried chilli flakes and sansho pepper, which is ground from the dried berries of a Japanese variety of prickly ash. Added to the mix are dried mandarin orange zest, black hemp seeds, white sesame seeds, white poppy seeds, and nori (seaweed) flakes.

Curry leaves

The leaves of the small tree *Murraya koenigii* (native to South and Southeast Asia) are used throughout southern India, Sri Lanka, and northern Thailand, as well as parts of Malaysia and in some Indonesian cooking. Curry leaves are best used fresh, but can be used dried if you cannot find fresh ones. Fresh curry leaves can be bought and stored in the freezer until needed. They impart a nutty, bitter taste to dishes, and smell of curry. Similarly to bay leaves, they are used for their flavour and aroma, but not eaten.

Tod man khao phad | Curried sweetcorn fritters

I was in a night market in southern Thailand when I first had these. I bought a bag of them straight from the hot oil and enjoyed eating them as I walked around. Before I knew it the bag was empty and I was in need of more. Almost on cue, a boy from the stall I had visited arrived with a tray, shouting out his wares in a singsong voice; I purchased another bag and continued on my way. They are great made with fresh corn, when the kernels are really sweet and the texture is crunchy. The curry paste in the batter makes these a great snack because they stimulate all the taste buds.

Serves 4–6

4 sweetcorn on the cob

4 tablespoons plain flour

4 tablespoons rice flour

2 tablespoons red or green Thai curry paste

1 tablespoon fish sauce such as nam pla

1 tablespoon light soy sauce

2 large eggs

¼ teaspoon salt

4 spring onions, finely chopped

handful of fresh Thai basil leaves or fresh coriander leaves, roughly chopped

vegetable oil for shallow-frying

freshly ground black pepper

1 Using a sharp knife, cut the kernels from the cobs of corn. Don't cut away too much of the lower end of the husk, nearest the core of the cob, as these kernels will be tougher. Put the two types of flour, curry paste, fish sauce, soy sauce, eggs, and the salt in a large mixing bowl. Season with black pepper. Mix together and add the corn kernels, spring onion, and basil or coriander. If the batter is a little dry, add about 2 tablespoons water, a little at a time – just enough until you have the right consistency.

2 Heat enough oil for shallow-frying in a large heavy pan over a medium-high heat. To test whether the oil is hot enough, drop a little of the batter into the oil – it should sizzle straight away. Take a tablespoon of the batter and carefully drop it into the hot oil, using the back of a metal spoon to flatten the batter to form a rough patty or cake. Repeat, cooking in batches of a few at a time, so that the temperature of the oil does not drop. Fry for 2–3 minutes on each side until golden and fragrant. When cooked, remove with a slotted spoon and drain on kitchen paper to soak up any excess oil.

3 Serve hot or at room temperature, with wedges of lime or a sour dipping sauce made with lime juice or rice vinegar (see p38). There will be a great balance of hot, sweet, and salty, set off and brought into balance by the sourness.

Partner with
Chilled seared tuna with ginger (pp120–1)
Tamarind beef with peanuts (pp180–1)

Chun juan | Prawn and chive spring rolls

Authentic spring rolls eaten as part of *dim sum* are fine and delicate. They should be no longer than a man's index finger and about twice as wide. Vary the filling according to what's available, maybe using a mix of seafood such as prawn, crab, scallop, or crayfish. They could be seasoned with spices and chilli, or be more herby.

1 Soak the rice vermicelli in boiling water until softened. Drain off the water, and finely chop the noodles so that they are 1–1.5cm (½–¾in) long. Combine the prawns with the noodles, and add the sesame oil, light soy sauce, and lemon juice. Season well with salt and black pepper. Add the chives and spring onion. Tear in the mint and coriander. Mix through.

2 Rice paper wrappers are very brittle, so they must be handled with care. Half-fill a large bowl with warm water. Lay out a clean damp tea towel on a clean work surface. Dip a rice paper wrapper in the warm water, and allow to soften for a few seconds. Gently shake off any excess liquid, then lay out on the cloth. Create a bit of a production line, and work on six or so wrappers at a time. When you have six discs laid out, spoon a tablespoon of mixture onto each one. Position it near the bottom edge of each disc, away from the edge.

3 Fold in the left edge, then the right edge, towards the centre, then tightly roll away from you. The roll should be compact and tight, rather like a short cigar about 8cm (3in) long. It is important to roll tightly – otherwise the roll will fall apart or explode when being fried. Set the finished roll on a plate or a tray. Continue until all the mixture has been used. The rolls can be assembled in advance and kept under cling film in the refrigerator for up to 4 hours before frying.

4 Heat the oil for deep-frying in a wok or a deep-sided frying pan over a medium-high heat. Fry the rolls in batches of a few at a time – they tend to stick to each other at the beginning. Cook for about 4 minutes until golden brown. Drain on kitchen paper, then serve hot. This recipe is well flavoured and juicy, so you do not need a dipping sauce, but the choice is yours.

Makes 16 rolls

120g (4oz) rice vermicelli

300g (10oz) cooked prawns, peeled and deveined, each cut into 3 pieces

1 tablespoon sesame oil

1 tablespoon light soy sauce

juice of ½ lemon

½ bunch of fresh chives, finely chopped

4 spring onions, finely chopped

30 fresh mint leaves

handful of fresh coriander, leaves picked

1 packet rice paper wrappers (available from Chinese supermarkets or Asian grocers)

400ml (14fl oz) vegetable oil for deep-frying

salt and freshly ground black pepper

Partner with
Sesame and ginger vinaigrette (p98)
Steamed barbecue pork buns (p101)

Murtabak | Spicy lamb-stuffed pancakes

The making of this fantastic stuffed pancake is one of the great sights of Singapore. *Murtabak* makers spin the dough around until it becomes an almost transparent sheet. Fillings for this savoury pastry range from egg and diced onion to this spicy meat version, or you could have one with cooked peas and pulses.

Serves 6

For the dough

200g (7oz) plain flour

1 teaspoon sugar

½ teaspoon salt

2 tablespoons butter, softened

60ml (2fl oz) milk

60ml (2fl oz) warm water

For the filling

2 tablespoons oil

2 onions, finely chopped

2 garlic cloves, finely chopped

2cm (¾in) piece of fresh root ginger, finely chopped

½ teaspoon ground turmeric

½ teaspoon chilli powder

2 teaspoons garam masala

2 tablespoons ground cumin

300g (10oz) lean lamb mince

1 fresh green chilli, deseeded and finely chopped

1 small bunch of fresh coriander, leaves picked and roughly chopped

3 eggs, beaten

1 tablespoon vegetable oil or melted butter for cooking

salt and freshly ground black pepper

1 Mix the flour, sugar, and salt in a large bowl. Rub in the butter using your fingertips, then mix in the liquid until you have a soft, pliable dough. Turn out onto a lightly floured work surface. Knead for 10 minutes until smooth and elastic. Divide into six balls. Lightly oil a clean bowl and the dough balls. Leave to rest, covered, for 1 hour.

2 Meanwhile, prepare the filling. Heat the oil in a heavy pan over a medium-high heat. Gently sweat half of the onion for 4–5 minutes until soft. Add the garlic and ginger. Sauté for 1 minute, then add the dried spices. Cook for a further minute until fragrant, to combine the flavours. Add the lamb, and season well with salt and black pepper. Stir-fry for about 5 minutes until the meat is browned. Remove from the heat, and transfer to a shallow dish to cool. Once cool, stir in the remaining onion, chopped chilli, and coriander. Check the seasoning. Roughly divide the mixture into six equal portions.

3 To shape the *murtabak*, lightly oil a work surface. Take a dough ball and, with the palm of your hand, flatten it out. Using an oiled rolling pin and your fingers, gently stretch out the ball until it is a thin disc about 30cm (12in) in diameter. Smear some beaten egg over the disc, then place a portion of the filling in the centre. Fold the sides over, and wrap the *murtabak* neatly, as you would a square parcel.

4 Heat a heavy frying pan or griddle pan over a medium-high heat. Drizzle in a tablespoon of oil or melted butter. Gently transfer a pastry parcel to the pan, and cook for 3–4 minutes on each side until crisp and golden brown. Keep warm while you cook the remaining *murtabak*. If serving a lot of people, cut the *murtabak* into 4cm (1¾in) squares, and serve on a large central platter.

Goenmande | Pork and cabbage dumplings

The combination of pork, cabbage, and black pepper in these little fried dumplings from Korea is delicious. They are served with a dipping sauce of vinegar, sesame oil, and garlic, and are a great way to start an Asian meal.

1 To make the dipping sauce, crush the garlic with salt and sugar to form a smooth paste. Add the liquids and mix together.

2 Heat the 2 tablespoons oil in a heavy pan over a medium-high heat. Sauté the garlic and ginger for 2 minutes until fragrant. Add the pork and continue to sauté, stirring, for 5 minutes until the meat has browned.

3 Next add the shredded cabbage to the pan with the soy sauce, some salt, and some black pepper. Reduce the heat and cover the pan. Braise for about 5 minutes until the cabbage has wilted, but still has a little bite. Taste the pork and cabbage – it should be hot from the black pepper. Adjust the seasoning if necessary, then remove the pan from the heat and leave to cool. Once cool, add the spring onion and mix together.

4 Lay out six wonton wrappers at a time, and place 2 teaspoons of pork and cabbage mixture on each wrapper. Brush the edges with a little water, and fold over to make a half-moon. Squeeze the edges tightly closed, using your thumb and finger to press out any air bubbles. Cover with a damp cloth until ready to cook.

5 Heat the extra oil for shallow-frying in a heavy pan over a medium-high heat. Test the oil to see that it is hot enough before starting – a crumb of bread should start to sizzle straight away. Fry the dumplings in batches of six at a time so that the oil does not drop in temperature while they are cooking. Drain on kitchen paper. Serve hot, accompanied by the dipping sauce.

Makes 18

2 tablespoons vegetable oil plus 100ml (3½fl oz) extra for shallow-frying

2 garlic cloves, finely chopped

4cm (1¾in) piece of fresh root ginger, finely chopped

500g (1lb 2oz) pork mince

½ Chinese cabbage, heart removed and leaves shredded

2 tablespoons light soy sauce

4 spring onions, finely chopped

18 round wonton wrappers (available from Asian grocers)

salt and lots of freshly ground black pepper

For the dipping sauce

1 garlic clove

½ teaspoon salt

½ teaspoon sugar

2 tablespoons rice vinegar

2 tablespoons water

2 tablespoons sesame oil

Partner with
Miso soup with seven-spice chicken (pp96–7)
Sichuan spicy pickled cucumber (p152)

Iri goma tempura | Sesame tempura

Tempura is a light style of Japanese batter, which crisps very well with the minimum amount of cooking. It lends itself very well to shellfish and fresh asparagus because they remain very tender and still firm inside. This technique can be used for other vegetables, too. Soft-shell crabs are absolutely delicious to eat, and definitely worth tracking down if you have never had them before.

Serves 6

vegetable oil for deep-frying

plain flour for dredging

3 soft-shell crabs, cut in half (available fresh or frozen from a fishmonger or Asian grocers)

18 raw king prawns, peeled but with tails left intact

6 spring onions, trimmed and cut in half

9 fresh asparagus spears, cut to the same size as the spring onions

salt and freshly ground black pepper

1 quantity *ponzu* (see p122) or other dipping sauce of your choice, to serve

Sesame tempura batter

75g (2½oz) cornflour

100g (3½oz) self-raising flour

3 tablespoons sesame seeds

1 teaspoon sea salt

375ml (12fl oz) iced water

Partner with
Marinated barbecue beef (pp52–3)
Asian salad with pea shoots and sprouts (pp140–1)

1 To make the tempura batter, put the cornflour, self-raising flour, sesame seeds, and sea salt in a bowl. Whisk in the iced water, and mix together to form a slightly lumpy batter, rather than a smooth one – tempura batter should have small lumps of dried flour.

2 Half-fill a large high-sided pan with vegetable oil for deep-frying, and heat over a medium-high heat until 180°C (350°F). To check whether the oil is the right temperature, simply fry a small piece of bread – it should turn golden in about 15 seconds. Season the plain flour with salt and black pepper.

3 Start with the halved soft-shell crabs. Dredge in the seasoned flour, then dip in the batter. Shake off any excess and lower the crab into the batter. Be careful not to splash the hot oil. Deep-fry for 3–4 minutes until golden brown, turning once during cooking. Drain on kitchen paper. Repeat the battering process with the prawns. Deep-fry the prawns for 2 minutes until they are pale golden, cooking in batches so that the temperature of the oil does not drop. Drain on kitchen paper. Lastly, batter and deep-fry the spring onion and asparagus in the same way. Cook for 1–2 minutes so that they are still crunchy and not overcooked.

4 Serve everyone a selection of each type of tempura. Have either individuals bowls of the *ponzu* dipping sauce (p122) or another dipping sauce alongside each serving, or place one bowl in the centre of the table. Remember that the sauce needs to have salty, sour, and hot elements to cut the sweet richness of the fresh shellfish, spring onion, and asparagus.

Ngephe gyaw | Burmese turmeric fishcakes

Burma has a long southern coastline on the Andaman Sea and is rich in all kinds of fish and seafood. These fishcakes use a combination of fish and prawns. You could use a few types of fish, or fish and prawns, crab, or squid. All these choices would be authentic, as the seafood in this region is so bounteous. The use of turmeric and ground ginger shows that this is a recipe with origins in India.

Serves 6

500g (1lb 2oz) firm white fish such as cod or snapper

1 teaspoon ground ginger

½ teaspoon ground red chilli flakes

1 garlic clove

3 shallots

300g (10oz) uncooked prawns, peeled and deveined

handful of fresh coriander, leaves picked

1 tablespoon fish sauce such as nam pla

1 teaspoon ground turmeric

250ml (8fl oz) vegetable oil

salt and freshly ground black pepper

1 Remove the skin and bones from the fish, and cut into 3cm (1¼in) dice. Put the ginger, chilli, garlic, and shallot into a food processor, and pulse to make a rough pulp. Add the prawns and fish to the food processor with the coriander and fish sauce. Continue to work until a smooth, well-combined paste forms. (Do not add the turmeric at this stage because it will dye the food processor orange.)

2 Transfer the fish paste to a metal bowl. Add the turmeric and mix with your hands until the paste is orange, to ensure the turmeric is evenly combined with the rest of the fish mixture. Season with salt and black pepper. Mix through.

3 Moisten your hands with a little water. Roll the fish mixture into 7cm (3in) sausages about 2.5cm (1in) thick. Heat the vegetable oil in a large pan or wok until hot. Fry a few of the fishcakes, adding one at a time. The fishcakes will expand, so do not add too many to the hot oil at one time. Fry for 4–5 minutes until golden brown, then drain on kitchen paper. Serve hot with a chilli dipping sauce.

Partner with
Grilled beef patties with shallots and cumin (pp26–7)
Pickled daikon salad with fried garlic (p142)

Appam | Rice flour pancakes

Appam are traditionally cooked in a sort of high, round-sided omelette pan called a *kuali*. The thick batter is swirled around the pan so that it forms thin lacy edges. Serve as suggested here, or eat plain to accompany a meal instead of rice. Or try them as a sweet snack, sprinkled with brown sugar and grated fresh coconut or sliced bananas.

1 Dissolve the yeast and sugar in the warm water, and leave for 10 minutes until the mixture starts to froth. Meanwhile, put the rice flour and coarser ground rice in a food processor. With the motor running, gradually add half the coconut cream to form a smooth dough. Add the yeast mixture to the dough and mix together, then transfer to a large bowl. Cover the dough and leave to rise in a warm place for 1 hour until it has doubled in size.

2 When the dough is ready, stir the salt into the remaining coconut cream, then mix the coconut cream into the dough to form a batter the thickness of double cream. The batter is now ready to use, or if you like it can be refrigerated for couple of hours until needed.

3 Heat a small omelette pan until quite hot over a medium-high heat. Grease the bottom and sides of the pan with oil, then tip out the excess to be used for the next pancake. Gently drop in a large ladleful of batter and, holding the pan in both hands and using an oven cloth, swirl the batter around so that it rides up and sticks to the sides of the pan. Tip any excess batter back into the bowl. Cover the pan with a lid, and reduce the heat to low to steam the centre of the pancake for 1 minute.

4 If you are making the *appam* with fried eggs, crack an egg into the centre of the pancake. Season with salt and black pepper, if using, and again cover the pan – this time for 3 minutes. The lacy edges of the *appam* should be golden brown and crisp; the centre of the egg perfectly cooked. Repeat the process with the other pancakes. Serve immediately with some chilli relish or sambal (see pp33, 45, and 89). Alternatively, if not using eggs, try one of the suggestions listed above.

Makes 6–8

2 teaspoons fresh yeast

1 teaspoon sugar

125ml (4fl oz) warm water

200g (7oz) rice flour

200g (7oz) ground rice

500ml (16fl oz) coconut milk

½ teaspoon salt

a little vegetable oil for greasing

6–8 eggs (optional)

salt and freshly ground black pepper (optional)

Partner with
Gujarati aubergine fritters (pp82–3)
Tomato chutney with green chilli (p179)

Ringrah na bhajia | Gujarati aubergine fritters

Gujarat, in northwestern India, is home to vibrant vegetarian dishes made to ancient recipes. Chickpeas and pulses are grown and used fresh, and ground into flour that makes noodles, breads, and batters. Make lots of these smoky fritters because everyone will keep coming back for more.

Serves 6–8

3 aubergines

300g (10oz) cooked chickpeas, drained and rinsed (you can use canned chickpeas)

2 tablespoons rice flour

1 tablespoon plain flour

½ teaspoon baking powder

4 spring onions, finely chopped

2 fresh hot green chillies, deseeded and finely chopped

3 garlic cloves, finely chopped

1 teaspoon ground cinnamon

½ teaspoon cayenne pepper

handful of fresh coriander, leaves picked and roughly chopped

2 eggs

vegetable oil for frying

sea salt and freshly ground black pepper

For the spiced yoghurt

1 teaspoon ground coriander

1 teaspoon ground cumin

200g (7oz) Greek-style yoghurt

½ teaspoon cayenne pepper

20 fresh coriander leaves, roughly chopped

juice of ½ lemon

1 Heat an overhead grill until very hot, and char the aubergines all over until the skin is blistered and the aubergines are soft inside. Remove from the grill and leave to cool. Once the aubergines are cool, peel off the skin and discard. Chop the flesh, and set aside.

2 To make the spiced yoghurt, roast the ground coriander and cumin seeds in a dry frying pan for 1–2 minutes until fragrant. Leave to cool, then stir into the yoghurt with the cayenne pepper. Season with salt and black pepper. Mix the coriander with the lemon juice, add to the yoghurt mixture, and stir through.

3 Put the drained chickpeas in a large bowl. Roughly mash with the two flours and the baking powder. Add the chopped aubergine, spring onion, chilli, and garlic, and stir through, then add the cinnamon, cayenne pepper, and chopped coriander. Season with salt and black pepper. Lightly beat the eggs and add to the bowl. Using a metal spoon, combine the ingredients into a batter.

4 To cook the fritters, heat a large heavy pan over a medium-high heat and add a couple of tablespoons of oil for cooking. First, fry a little piece of the mixture, and taste to check the seasoning. If necessary, adjust the seasoning and chilli content to suit your taste. Cooking in batches so that you don't crowd the pan and allow the temperature of the oil to drop, carefully spoon tablespoons of batter into the pan. Shallow-fry for 2–3 minutes, turning once during the cooking time, until the fritters are golden brown and cooked through. Drain on kitchen paper, and serve hot with the spiced yoghurt.

Keynotes | **Chillies**

If you were to sum up a cuisine in one word, "hot" could be one of those used for many Asian cuisines. This heat is largely associated with the chilli (*Capsicum frutescens*). It was only after the Portuguese and Spanish had been to South America in the 16th century, however, that this mighty plant was introduced to Asia.

Before the introduction of chilli to Asian food, much of the heat of the cuisine came from white pepper and spices such as ginger and garlic. In Thai cooking, if you come across a recipe made with white pepper, it is often an old Siamese recipe predating the arrival of chillies in the cuisine.

There is more vitamin C in chillies than in oranges, and they are also addictive. The heat from the chilli forces the body to release endorphins to deal with it, thus making you feel good. The more you eat, the more your tolerance for the heat increases.

Abundant variety

There are many varieties of chilli used across Asia – fresh and dried, large and small, red and green. All these chillies have unique tastes, so it is important to try to match the right ones to the dishes that you are going to make. The heat in the chilli

Green chilli

Dried red chilli

Fresh red chillies

Sambal oelek

comes from the seeds and the central core of white pith. The smaller the chilli, the hotter it is – bird's-eye chillies are an example of this. Large finger-length red (ripe) and green (unripe) chillies are usually moderately hot. Another important factor is that the hotter the climate where the chillies are grown, the riper and therefore the hotter the chilli will be.

> "The heat in the chilli comes from the seeds and the central core of white pith. The smaller the chilli, the hotter it is. Large finger-length red (ripe) and green (unripe) chillies are usually moderately hot."

In India, chillies are mostly used fresh in their green unripe state, but are still fiery hot. If you make a green masala paste or a curry from South India using fresh green chilli, it is likely to be very spicy. Most of the ripe red chillies that are grown are dried, with much of them being ground into chilli powder.

As you head further south throughout tropical Asia, the temperature increases – as does the spiciness of the food. This is true in India, Sri Lanka, Thailand, Malaysia, and Vietnam, to name but a few. You eat the hot food to make you sweat, which in turn cools you down. Also, there is much more sweet fruit and nuts such as coconut, papaya, mango and watermelon in the tropics. These are used to diffuse anything that is too hot.

Different approaches
In Thailand, the main chillies (*prik*) that are used are the finger-length varieties and also the tiny but fiery hot bird's-eye chilli, which can be red, orange, yellow, or green. A Thai condiment that is present on every communal table is *nam pla prik*, a simple concoction of sliced small chillies that is known as *prik khii nuu* (which translates slightly alarmingly as "mouse-dropping chillies"), floating in *nam pla* (Thai fish sauce). To make a dipping sauce for seafood, minced garlic, lime juice, and a little sugar are added – this is called *nam jim*. Similar condiments are used in Vietnam, Malaysia, and Indonesia.

Chillies can be pickled or preserved, or dry-roasted to impart a distinct smoky taste. Unripe green chillies have a sharp heat and a slightly acidic taste. When you want to lessen the heat of dried chillies, but without reducing flavour, cut them open and remove the seeds, then soak the dried skin in boiling water for 20 minutes before using. Always wash your hands well after handling chillies, before touching eyes, lips, and other sensitive areas.

Sambals

Throughout Malaysia, Indonesia, and Singapore, the sambal rules the table. This fiery chilli paste is served as a condiment and can be eaten on the side or spread on particular ingredients (see pp88–9). There are as many sambals, and as many techniques for making them, as there are chefs who use them. Some sambals call for fresh red chilli, while others use dried. A couple use green chilli (see pp44–5). Some are raw; others are fried. At the simplest end of the scale is *sambal oelek*, a combination of chilli, salt, and vinegar. It can be bought in jars and is a good base to start with. Shallots, garlic, galangal, and balachan (shrimp paste) can be added, as well as tamarind pulp and other spices. *Sambal ikan bilis* is made with small dried anchovies, while *sambal blachan* is a blend of chillies and shrimp paste.

Ban khoai | Happy crêpes

The combination of textures of crispy, soft, and chewy found in this recipe, as well as the grouping of flavours, is very typical of Vietnamese cuisine. Happy crêpes are great at any time of the day. It is a good idea to have a couple of skillets on the go, so that you can produce a continuous flow of these fantastic crêpes. They gained their name from the great noise they make when they are cooking.

Serves 4

120g (4oz) rice flour

60g (2oz) cornflour

30g (1oz) plain flour

3 spring onions, white and green parts sliced separately

250g (9oz) pork mince

2 tablespoons fish sauce such as nuoc nam

2 garlic cloves, finely chopped

250g (9oz) raw prawns, peeled, deveined, and roughly chopped

vegetable oil for cooking

250g (9oz) beansprouts, rinsed and trimmed

1 small onion, finely sliced

10 large button mushrooms, finely sliced

3 eggs, beaten

freshly ground black pepper

1 Combine the rice flour, cornflour, and plain flour with the spring onion whites and 560ml (17fl oz) water to make a smooth batter the consistency of double cream. Combine the pork with half the fish sauce, half the chopped garlic, and half the spring onion greens. Season with black pepper.

2 Mix the prawns with the remaining fish sauce, garlic, and spring onion greens. Again, season with black pepper. Arrange in bowls with all the other ingredients to hand near the stove.

3 Heat a small skillet or omelette pan over a medium-high heat. Add a tablespoon of oil. Into the hot pan, put a tablespoon of minced pork and two or three pieces of prawn; cook for 2 minutes.

4 Reduce the heat to medium, and add 3 tablespoons batter. Add a tablespoon of the beansprouts and a few slices of onion and mushroom. Cover with a lid, and cook for 2 minutes. Remove the lid, and add 3 tablespoons beaten egg. Cover once again, and cook for a further 2 minutes.

5 Fold the omelette in half, and carry on cooking until the underside is really crisp and golden, then turn over and cook on the other side until golden, too, allowing about 2 minutes for each side. Keep the process going, so that you are serving a stream of crêpes, rather than a batch at the end. Serve each happy crêpe immediately, accompanied by *nuoc dau phung* (see p153), a Vietnamese peanut dipping sauce.

Partner with
Sesame chicken salad with white pepper (pp118–19)
Vietnamese peanut dipping sauce (p153)

Taruang balado | Sumatran aubergine sambal

There are many variations of sambals, the fiery hot chilli pastes used in Indonesian and Malaysian cuisine. Some use dried chillies, while others use fresh. Some sambals, such as this one, are completely vegetarian, while others use shrimp paste, fish sauce, or dried fish. So many islands and different cultures make up Indonesia that it is not really surprising that there is such a melting pot of food styles and ancient culinary influences. You can easily make a larger batch of the sambal and keep it in the refrigerator to use in stir-fries, noodles, and seafood dishes.

1 To make the sambal paste, halve the tomatoes and remove the seeds. Put a tomato half in the palm of your hand, with the flesh side outermost. Using a cheese grater, grate the tomato flesh into a bowl, leaving the leftover skin in your hand. Continue until you have grated all the tomato halves, and discard the skin.

2 Using a mortar and pestle, crush the chilli with the garlic and salt to make a paste. Add the shallot, and continue to pound to make a smooth purée. Heat the 2 tablespoons oil in a heavy pan over a medium-high heat. Add the chilli paste, and fry for 4–5 minutes until fragrant. Add the grated tomato pulp, and cook for a further 2–3 minutes until softened and combined. Season with salt and black pepper, and add the lime juice and 2 tablespoons water. Set aside.

3 Cut the aubergines in half lengthways. Heat the 3 tablespoons oil in a heavy pan over a medium-high heat. Fry the aubergines in batches for about 3 minutes on each side until tender and golden brown. Season with salt and black pepper.

4 Spread the sambal paste on the cut side of the aubergines and transfer to a serving dish. Serve with lime wedges as part of a larger selection of dishes.

Serves 4

750g (1lb 10oz) finger aubergines

3 tablespoons vegetable oil

salt and freshly ground
  black pepper

lime wedges, to serve

For the sambal paste

2 large tomatoes

5 fresh red chillies, deseeded and
  finely chopped

2 garlic cloves, finely chopped

1 teaspoon salt

5 shallots, finely chopped

2 tablespoons vegetable oil

juice of 1 lime

Partner with
Minced pork balls with
garlic and pepper (pp38–9)
Crisp peanut wafers (p65)
Malay beef rendang (pp148–9)

Pe chan gyaw | Burmese spiced split pea fritters

The split peas, cumin seeds, and coriander seeds found in these simple Burmese fritters demonstrate the recipe's original roots in India. Yet, despite the influence on Burmese cuisine of its neighbours India, China, and Thailand, it remains unique and quite distinctive. Serve these fritters with drinks or at the start of a meal.

Serves 6

100g (3½ oz) dried yellow split peas, picked and rinsed

1 tablespoon coriander seeds

1 tablespoon cumin seeds

2 garlic cloves

½ teaspoon crushed dried red chilli flakes

1 tablespoon vegetable oil plus 250ml (8fl oz) extra for deep-frying

4 shallots, finely chopped

5 tablespoons rice flour

salt and freshly ground black pepper

1 Soak the dried split peas in plenty of cold water overnight, then drain off the soaking liquid and rinse the split peas under fresh cold water until the water runs clear.

2 Using a mortar and pestle, crush the coriander and cumin seeds until fine. Add the garlic and chilli flakes, and continue to pound to make a paste. Heat the 1 tablespoon oil in a small saucepan over a medium-high heat, and add the spice and garlic paste. Fry for 2 minutes until fragrant. Reduce the heat to low, add the shallot, and continue to fry until the shallot is soft and just starting to caramelize. Remove from the heat.

3 Mix the flour and 500ml (16fl oz) water in a bowl to make a batter. Add the soaked split peas and the shallot mixture, and season with salt and black pepper. Heat the extra vegetable oil for deep-frying in a wok or high-sided heavy pan. When the oil is hot, test a little piece of the batter – it should sizzle immediately. Fry for about 2 minutes until golden brown. Remove from the oil and, when cooled slightly, taste the fritter and adjust the seasoning, if necesary. The batter may need some more salt and pepper.

4 When the seasoning is right, carefully spoon tablespoons of the batter into the hot oil, and deep-fry for 2–3 minutes until crisp and golden. Deep-fry only a few fritters at a time, and remove from the oil with a slotted spoon before draining on kitchen paper. Keep frying in batches until all the batter has been used. Serve hot.

Partner with
Isaan-style grilled chicken (pp40–1)
Sri Lankan smoky aubergine dip (pp150–1)

Hot and steamy

There is something supremely comforting about food that has been slow-cooked, simmered, or steamed, to be brought to the table for you to enjoy. It can also be supremely tasty, benefiting from the addition of spices and condiments that lift the food from mere comfort eating into something singular to savour. Chinese dim sum steamed dumplings, hot spicy soups, a sumptuous pilaf from the culinary treasure trove of what was once the Persian empire – these dishes range from what may be familiar favourites to the more exotic.

Taugeh masak kerang | Fried bean sprouts and clams

The sweetness of clams and mussels, as well as the ease of cooking them, makes them a favourite in any coastal region where their freshness can be assured. This very simple dish consists of only a few ingredients, but the flavours are fantastic. Roll up your sleeves and get stuck in – there really is no polite way of eating this.

Serves 4

1kg (2¼lb) clams, scrubbed and cleaned

3cm (1¼in) piece of fresh root ginger

3 celery sticks, white central part of stem only

3 tablespoons vegetable oil

2 fresh red chillies, deseeded and finely chopped

3 garlic cloves, any green inner shoot removed, thinly sliced

400g (14oz) beansprouts, trimmed and rinsed

1 tablespoon soy sauce

juice of 1 lime

1 small bunch of fresh coriander, leaves picked

salt and freshly ground black pepper

1 Rinse the clams under plenty of cold running water. Remove any dirt or barnacles with an old knife. Keep rinsing until the water is completely clear. Discard any clams that do not close when they are tapped on the work surface, as they are dead. Also remove any that smell or have broken shells. Cut the ginger into thin slices, then finely shred into thin matchsticks. Set aside. Cut the celery into 4cm (1¾in) lengths, then cut these into matchsticks as well. Set aside.

2 Heat a heavy pan over a medium-high heat. Add half of the oil, and fry half each of the chilli, garlic, and ginger for 1–2 minutes until fragrant. Add the clams and a splash of water to steam. Cover with a lid and cook over a high heat, shaking the pan occasionally, for 2 minutes. Remove the lid, and stir the contents from the bottom. Cook for a further 2 minutes until the clams have all opened (discard any that do not). Set a colander lined with a clean piece of muslin or cheesecloth (or even a suitable clean dish cloth) over a bowl. Strain the clams, trapping any specks of grit or sand in the cloth, and reserve the strained cooking liquor.

3 Heat a wok over a medium-high heat, and add the remaining oil. Fry the remaining chilli, garlic, and ginger for 1 minute until fragrant. Add the celery, and stir-fry for a further minute. Next, add the beansprouts, and stir-fry vigorously for 1 minute. Finally, add the cooked clams, reserved cooking liquor, soy sauce, and lime juice. Season with plenty of black pepper, and stir in the coriander leaves. Taste the juice and adjust the seasoning. It may need a little salt or may be just right. The juice will be hot, sweet, salty, and sour. Stir through, and serve in prepared bowls with all the tempting juices.

Partner with
Marinated grilled mackerel (pp22–3)
Burmese spiced split pea fritters (pp90–1)

Miso shiru | Miso soup with seven-spice chicken

Miso is a paste made from fermented soya beans and a grain – either barley or rice. It is aged for up to three years to mellow the flavours. There are about six basic types, ranging in texture and colour from pale yellow to a deep chocolate brown; all have a wonderful savoury taste. It comes in all manner of packaging. If you can, try to use the product that is the least commercially processed, as the taste will be superior. Miso provides a delicious base for a soup to which you can add any number of ingredients – mushrooms, seafood, grilled meat, or simply tofu.

1 Heat a ridged cast-iron grill pan until very hot. Season the chicken breasts with salt, black pepper, and the shichimi togarashi. Grill the chicken until golden brown and cooked on both sides, allowing about 4 minutes on each side depending on the size.

2 Bring the dashi stock to the boil, add the miso paste, and gently dissolve, before removing from the heat. Add the spring onion, ginger, and soy sauce to the stock.

3 Cut the grilled chicken into slices, and divide into 4 portions. Place a portion each in the bottom of 4 serving bowls. Pour over the stock, making sure to divide the ginger and spring onion evenly between each serving. Serve immediately, with extra soy sauce if required. There will be a balance between the sweet chicken and the hot spices and ginger. The stock will be sour from the miso and salty from the bonito flakes and soy sauce. The kombu, meanwhile, works as a flavour enhancer, intensifying all the flavours on your taste buds.

Dashi stock Put a 6 x 4cm (2½ x 1¾in) piece of dried kombu (kelp) in a pan, and cover with 1.5 litres (2¾ pints) water. Bring to the boil, uncovered. Just before the water starts boiling, remove the kombu and discard. Sprinkle in 50g (1¾oz) bonito flakes, and remove the pan from the heat. When the flakes have sunk to the bottom of the pan, strain the liquid and discard the bonito flakes. You now have a basic stock that can be flavoured with light soy sauce, rice wine, ginger, or mushrooms.

Serves 4

2 large skinless chicken breast fillets, about 400g (14oz) in total

½ teaspoon shichimi togarashi (Japanese seven-spice) (available from Japanese or Asian grocers)

1 litre (1¾ pints) dashi stock (see below)

40g (1½oz) miso paste (available from Japanese grocers and health food shops)

4 spring onions, finely chopped

4cm (1¾in) piece of fresh root ginger, cut into matchsticks

2 tablespoons light soy sauce plus extra if needed

salt and freshly ground black pepper

Partner with
Steamed barbecue pork buns (p101)
Sashimi of sea bream with hot dressing (p143)

Har gau | Steamed prawn wontons

What I love about eating dim sum is the huge selection of tasty morsels that are brought to your table in a seeming never-ending flow. Here, wonton pastry wrappers are used; these are made from a soft egg pastry. Water chestnuts are available fresh, frozen, and canned from Asian grocers. The canned version is sufficient for this dish. You can vary the filling to suit your taste.

Serves 6

6 water chestnuts, peeled

3 spring onions, finely chopped

1 small bunch of fresh chives, finely chopped

¼ teaspoon dried red chilli flakes

2 teaspoons sesame oil

2 tablespoons vegetable oil

1 tablespoon light soy sauce

500g (1lb 2oz) peeled and deveined cooked prawns, roughly chopped

1 packet won ton wrappers (available from most Chinese or Asian grocers)

½ teaspoon salt

egg wash for sealing pastry

freshly ground black pepper

1 quantity sesame and ginger vinaigrette (see right), to serve

1 Rinse the chestnuts under cold running water, then finely chop. Mix together in a bowl with the spring onion and chives. Season well with salt and black pepper, and add the dried chilli, sesame oil, vegetable oil, and soy sauce. Stir through to mix well, and leave to stand for 20 minutes before adding the prawns.

2 Using a pastry cutter, cut the wrappers into a 6cm (2¼in) circles. Only do six or seven at a time – otherwise the pastry will dry out. Place a spoonful of chestnut filling on each piece, then fold over to form a half-moon. Brush the edges with egg wash, and press together tightly to seal, making sure that no air bubbles are present.

3 Place the wontons on greaseproof paper and transfer, paper and all, to a bamboo steamer over boiling water. Steam for 10 minutes. Carefully lift the wontons off the paper and serve immediately, accompanied by the sesame and ginger vinaigrette.

Sesame and ginger vinaigrette This dressing is delicious with all manner of food, from wontons and dim sum dumplings, to rare grilled tuna or seared cubes of beef. Mix together the grated zest and juice of 1 orange, ½ tablespoon grated fresh root ginger, ½ teaspoon crushed dried red chilli flakes, and ½ teaspoon sugar. Add to the juice of 1 lime, 1 tablespoon rice wine vinegar, 1 tablespoon light soy sauce, 3 tablespoons sesame oil, and 2 tablespoons light vegetable oil (such as peanut or olive oil) in a glass jar with a tight-fitting lid. Season with salt and black pepper. Shake well, then check the seasoning. Make sure that all the flavours are blended and that no one in particular overpowers the balance. You could use fresh chilli if desired. The dressing keeps in the refrigerator for at least a week.

Partner with
Chinese barbecue spare ribs (pp24–5)
Spring onion and chive flower rolls (p110–11)

Chuan wei hun tun | Sichuan chicken dumplings

Sichuan cooking is famed for its spiciness. Among the ingredients used to achieve this are Sichuan peppercorns. Although called pepper, they are actually dried berries from the flowering shrub called *fagara*. Sichuan pepper should be a mid red-brown and has a sharp lemony taste which causes a slight numbing to the tongue.

Makes 30 dumplings

200g (7oz) fresh spinach, leaves picked

½ teaspoon ground Sichuan peppercorns (see note)

½ teaspoon ground white pepper

2 tablespoons vegetable oil

100g (3½oz) beansprouts, rinsed and trimmed

1 teaspoon salt

300g (10oz) minced chicken

1 egg, lightly beaten

4cm (1¾in) piece of fresh root ginger, finely chopped

2 tablespoons Shaoxing rice wine

30 wonton wrappers

For the hot sauce

1 garlic clove

½ teaspoon sugar

4 tablespoons light soy sauce

½ teaspoon ground cinnamon

2 tablespoons chilli oil

1 tablespoon rice vinegar

3 spring onions, finely sliced

Partner with
Sichuan peppered beef (pp170–1)
Fried aubergine with toasted sesame seeds (p178)

1 To make the hot sauce, use a mortar and pestle to crush the garlic and sugar to a smooth paste. Mix with the remaining ingredients. Set aside. Rinse the spinach in cold water two or three times. Leave to drain in a colander, shaking to remove any excess water. Mix together the Sichuan and ground white pepper.

2 Heat the oil in a wok over a medium-high heat. Stir-fry the spinach and beansprouts until wilted. Season with some of the salt and mixed ground pepper. Remove from the heat, and let cool. Combine the chicken with the egg, ginger, rice wine, and remaining salt and mixed ground pepper. Drain the spinach and beansprouts, turn out onto a board, and roughly chop. Combine with the chicken mixture. Fry a little mixture to taste; adjust the seasoning if necessary.

3 Lay out six wonton wrappers at a time on a clean work surface. Put a heaped teaspoon of chicken mixture onto the centre of each wrapper. Brush the edges of the wrappers with a little water. Fold over on a diagonal, and press the edges together. Squeeze the excess air out, away from the dumpling filling. The wontons will be triangular, with the round filling on the inside. Wet your finger and thumb, and press two of the triangle points together; hold for a few seconds until they stick. You will now have a shape that is like a tortellini. Repeat until all the wonton wrappers are used.

4 Bring a large pan of water to the boil. Simmer the dumplings for 2–3 minutes. Drain with a slotted spoon over a clean tea towel, put into serving bowls, and spoon over the sauce. Serve at once.

Note Before grinding, roast the Sichuan peppercorns in a dry frying pan over a medium heat for 2–3 minutes until fragrant.

Char siu bao | Steamed barbecue pork buns

A Chinese staple, these buns are completely addictive. The hot, pillow-like dough is broken open to reveal the sweet pork drenched in rich sauce. These steamed gems are frequently served as part of a larger selection of dim sum. They can be prepared in advance, then steamed when required.

1 To make the dough, put the sugar and water into a mixing bowl. Stir until the sugar has dissolved. Add the yeast, and leave for 10 minutes until it is frothy. Add the oil and baking powder, and sift in the flour. Stir the mixture with your hands, until it comes together as a smooth, slightly wet dough. Cover the bowl with a damp cloth, and allow the dough to rise for 40–60 minutes until it has doubled in size.

2 To make the pork filling, heat the two oils in a wok, and add the garlic, ginger, chilli, and mushroom. Stir-fry for 2–3 minutes until fragrant. Add the pork and spring onion, stir through, then add the remaining ingredients. Reduce the heat, and stir-fry for 2–3 minutes until the liquid has almost evaporated. Taste the mixture – it should be sweet from the meat and rich sauce, sour from the vinegar, hot from the chilli and ginger, and salty from the sesame oil and light soy sauce. Adjust the seasoning where appropriate, perhaps with a little lemon juice or black pepper. Remove from the heat and leave to cool.

3 Knock the air out of the dough with your hand, and scrape out of the bowl. You can either use the dough immediately or cover with cling film and put in the refrigerator. Use within 12 hours – otherwise the yeast will start to ferment. When ready, divide the dough into 12 balls. On a floured work surface, roll each ball into a neat disc about 8cm (3in) in diameter. Place a tablespoon of the pork mixture into the centre of each disc. Bring the edges up around the filling, and pinch together to seal tightly.

4 Line a bamboo steamer with a piece of greaseproof paper. Place the buns on the paper, allowing space for them to rise. Steam for 10–12 minutes, or until the tops of the buns have opened. Serve immediately while they are still piping hot.

Serves 6

- ½ tablespoon vegetable oil
- 1 teaspoon sesame oil
- 2 garlic cloves, finely chopped
- 3cm (1¼in) piece of fresh root ginger, finely chopped
- 1 fresh red chilli, deseeded and finely chopped
- 6 fresh oyster or shiitake mushrooms, diced
- 400g (14oz) Chinese barbecue pork (see p48, or available from Chinese grocers)
- 3 spring onions, finely chopped
- 1 tablespoon rice vinegar
- 1 teaspoon palm sugar or soft brown sugar
- 2 tablespoons hoisin sauce
- 1 tablespoon light soy sauce
- a little freshly squeezed lemon juice (optional)
- freshly ground black pepper

For the yeast bun dough

- 1 tablespoon caster sugar
- 250ml (8fl oz) lukewarm water
- 1½ teaspoons dried yeast
- 1 tablespoon vegetable oil
- 1½ teaspoons baking powder
- 400g (14oz) plain flour

Keynotes | **Rice and noodles**

Rice is such an important crop the world over, with half the population of the planet consuming it two or three times a day. China is credited with the earliest cultivation of this plant, dating back to Neolithic times. Thousands of varieties are grown throughout Asia, cooked in different ways and eaten during various seasons. Connossieurs claim that they can tell the difference in taste between rice harvested at different times, or the type of rice being cooked just by its smell. Despite the huge number of different varieties, two main types predominate: long-grain and short-grain rice.

Long-grain and short-grain rice

Long-grain rice is the most commonly used rice in India, China, Thailand, Vietnam, and throughout Southeast Asia. It cooks up into easily separated fluffy grains. Basmati rice is the most widely planted variety in India. With its silky texture and superior aroma, it is used for aromatic rice pilafs, birianis, and masala rice. Basmati is also the most exported of the Indian varieties of rice. In China, Vietnam, Thailand, and other parts of Southeast Asia, refreshingly fragrant jasmine long-grain rice is the most popular.

Short-grain rice is favoured in Japan and Korea because it has a shorter growing season and is ideal for eating with chopsticks. Slightly stickier than long-grain, short-grain rice is eaten with savoury dishes in Japan and Korea; in Southern China and Vietnam, it is commonly used for rice porridge.

Soba noodles

Black glutinous rice

Rice vermicelli

Basmati rice

Flat rice noodles

Rice paper wrappers

In Vietnam, rice paper wrappers are called *banh trang* and are used for Vietnamese spring and summer rolls, or wrapping meat or seafood. They can be fried or used fresh. To make the wrappers, a batter is made from rice flour, water, and salt. A pancake of this batter is then steamed, before being dried on bamboo mats in the sun. I went to

> "Noodles are intrinsic to life in many parts of Asia such as China, Japan, and Korea. They originated in China more than 2,000 years ago, and have been made commercially for centuries."

a village in Vietnam that made these, and the whole place was viewed through these white translucent discs – it was quite surreal. Rice paper wrappers are sold dried in packets of 50 or 100.

Rice noodles

Noodles are intrinsic to life in many parts of Asia such as China, Japan, and Korea. They originated in China more than 2,000 years ago, and have been made commercially for centuries. Fresh and dried noodles are available in all shapes and sizes.

Fresh rice noodles are called *fen* in China. There are four main sizes according to width: flat, round, fine, and very fine. They are eaten in a number of ways – stir-fried, in soups, or with a sauce.

Dried rice noodles are made much in the same way as rice paper, and are called "rice sticks". The thinnest variety is rice vermicelli, used in salads and cold dishes, or in stir-fries and soups. Other rice sticks are about 5mm (¼ in) wide like a ribbon and about the length of a chopstick. These are soaked in warm water before adding to soups or stir-fries.

Also made from rice flour, dried thick laksa noodles resemble spaghetti. There may be many variations of laksa, but the type of noodles used is pretty consistent throughout Malaysia and Singapore.

Other noodles

Fresh egg noodles, known as *mein* or Hokkien noodles, are made with wheat. Dried wheat noodles are also made, and either packed in lengths or rolled like a tight bird's nest. Cellophane noodles (*dong fen*) are made from mung bean flour. Transparent when cooked, they are often used in soups and salads. In Japan, egg noodles are called *ramen*, while soba noodles are made from buckwheat and mostly eaten in the north. They are usually pale brown, but some are green and flavoured with green tea. Round or flat udon noodles are made from wheat flour and are white in colour; they are readily available.

Glutinous rice

Glutinous rice is a type of short-grain rice that is often referred to as "sticky rice". The rice is first soaked for between 5 and 8 hours, then drained and steamed on a clean cloth or piece of muslin in a bamboo steamer for 30–40 minutes. The rice grains become thick, firm, and translucent. Glutinous rice is never really eaten on its own, but often mixed with savoury ingredients such as pork or mushrooms, or made into rice cakes that are wrapped in banana leaves. In Thai cooking, after the rice is steamed, it is mixed with thick coconut cream, sugar, and a pinch of salt, and served with ripe mango. When made with fresh coconut, this simple dish is really amazing.

Zarda pilau | Lamb pilaf with saffron and nuts

Pilaf is a spectacular way of cooking rice. Some pilafs are plain, while others are lavish and designed for special occasions and festivals. Spices used also vary enormously, depending on from where in the vast Persian empire the pilaf originated. Char masala is a blend of four spices in equal quantities: cinnamon, cloves, cumin, and black cardamom seeds. To make, grind the spices using a mortar and pestle, or a spice grinder. Grind only a small amount at a time, and store in an airtight container.

Serves 4

800g (1¾lb) leg of lamb

400g (14oz) basmati rice

3 tablespoons vegetable oil

2 onions, finely chopped

2 teaspoons char masala

2 bay leaves

2 tablespoons sugar

50g (1¾oz) flaked almonds

50g (1¾oz) skinless pistachio
   nuts

1 teaspoon saffron threads

salt and freshly ground
   black pepper

Partner with
Spiced stuffed
aubergine (p165)
Afghan new year
compote (p191)

1 Trim the lamb of excess fat and bone the meat (you can ask your butcher to do this for you). Dice the lamb into 2cm (¾in) cubes. Rinse the rice in several changes of cold water until the water runs clear, then leave to soak in fresh water for 30 minutes.

2 Meanwhile, heat the vegetable oil in a large casserole dish over a medium-high heat. Add the onion, and sauté for 5–6 minutes until soft and starting to caramelize and turn golden brown. Add the diced lamb and brown on all sides. Sprinkle in the char masala and bay leaves, and cover with 250ml (8fl oz) water. Season with salt and black pepper. Bring to the boil, then reduce to a simmer and cook for 30–40 minutes until the meat is tender. When the meat is ready, remove from the pan, together with the onion.

3 Put the sugar and 100ml (3½fl oz) water into a separate pan. Simmer for about 5 minutes until the sugar has dissolved and the liquid is syrupy. Add the almonds, pistachio nuts, and saffron.

4 Preheat the oven to 150°C (300°F/Gas 3). Bring 1.5 litres (2¾ pints) water to the boil in a clean pan. Drain the soaked rice, parboil for 3 minutes, then drain again in a large sieve. Mix a quarter of the rice into the syrup and nuts. Add the remaining rice to the meat juices in the casserole dish. Top one half of the rice in the casserole with the cooked lamb and the other half with the rice and nut mixture. Cover with a tight-fitting lid, and transfer to the oven. Slow-cook at this low temperature for 45 minutes. Serve the lamb pilaf on a large platter garnished with the nut-and-saffron-studded rice.

Mandu | Steamed green vegetable rolls

A delicious Korean version of the Chinese *char siu bao*, or steamed barbecue pork buns (see p101), these soft, pillowy rolls are filled a tempting mixture of cabbage and oyster mushrooms. They are eaten as a snack and also at the start of a larger meal consisting of many courses.

1 Heat the vegetable oil in a heavy pan over a medium-high heat. Add the garlic, ginger, dried chilli, and torn oyster mushrooms. Stir-fry for 2–3 minutes until the mushrooms are golden and the mixture is fragrant. Add the onion, and reduce the heat to medium. Sweat for 4–5 minutes until the onion is soft.

2 Add the cabbage, bok choy, and soy sauce. Season with salt and black pepper. Cover the pan with a lid, and sweat the cabbage over a low heat until soft, but still with a slight bite. Add the lemon juice and sesame oil. Remove from the heat, and turn out the contents of the pan onto a board. Roughly chop. Allow to cool before adding the spring onion.

3 Divide the prepared dough into 12 balls. On a floured work surface, roll each ball into a neat disc about 8cm (3in) in diameter. Place a tablespoon of the cooked cabbage mixture into the centre of each disc. Bring the edges of the dough up around the filling, and pinch them together to seal.

4 Line a bamboo steamer with a piece of greaseproof paper. Place the buns on the paper, allowing space for them to rise. Steam for 10–12 minutes, or until the tops of the buns have opened. Serve immediately while they are still piping hot.

Serves 6

½ tablespoon vegetable oil

2 garlic cloves, finely chopped

3cm (1¼in) piece of fresh root ginger, finely chopped

1 small dried red chilli, crushed

10 fresh oyster mushrooms, torn into equal pieces

2 onions, finely chopped

½ Chinese cabbage, finely sliced

2 heads of bok choy, finely sliced

1 tablespoon light soy sauce

juice of 1 lemon

1 teaspoon sesame oil

3 spring onions, finely chopped

salt and freshly ground black pepper

1 quantity yeast bun dough (see p101)

Partner with
Fresh lettuce cups with chicken (pp124–5)
Chilled soba noodles with seared salmon (pp130–1)

Jiaozi | Mushroom pot-sticker dumplings

These are a popular Chinese start to a meal. You can alter the filling to suit your taste, making them vegetarian, or perhaps using pork, beef, duck, or another combination. They are also very popular in Japan, where they are known as *gyoza*. The dumplings are first fried, before liquid is added to the pan, then finished off by steaming.

1 Soak the dried mushrooms in the boiling water for 15 minutes. Meanwhile, heat some of the oil in a heavy pan over a high heat. Fry a quarter of the field and oyster mushrooms for 4 minutes until well coloured, then remove from the pan and set aside. Repeat with the rest of the fresh mushrooms, cooking in batches. Set aside.

2 Drain the shiitake mushrooms and roughly chop, reserving the liquid. Heat a little more oil in the same pan over a medium-high heat; fry half of the garlic and ginger for 1 minute. Add the shiitake; fry for 3 minutes until browned. Strain the mushroom liquid through a fine sieve into the pan; cook for 3–4 minutes until absorbed. Add the reserved mushrooms. Season with the 1 teaspoon salt and some black pepper. Remove from the heat. Transfer to a chopping board.

3 Return the pan to a medium heat. Fry the remaining garlic and ginger in a little oil for 2 minutes until fragrant. Add the shallot, and sweat until soft. Chop the mushrooms to the same size. Return to the pan with the soy sauce, sesame oil, brown sugar, and black pepper. Cook for 3–4 minutes to combine the flavours. Allow to cool.

4 Lay out six wonton wrappers at a time, and place 2 teaspoons of mushroom mixture on each one. Brush the edges with a little water. Fold over to make a half-moon. Squeeze the edges tightly together using your thumb and forefinger, then press the base of each dumpling on the work surface so that they will sit upright while cooking. Heat a little oil in a large frying pan over a medium heat. Gently fry the dumplings, bottom-side down, for about 2 minutes until golden brown. Add the rice wine, cover with a lid, and reduce the heat. Steam for 3 minutes until all the liquid has been absorbed. Carefully remove and serve with the black vinegar dipping sauce.

Serves 4–6

12 dried shiitake mushrooms

100ml (3½fl oz) boiling water

about 4 tablespoons vegetable oil for cooking

250g (9oz) field mushrooms, cut into 3mm (⅛in) slices

250g (9oz) fresh oyster mushrooms, torn

3 garlic cloves, finely chopped

5cm (2in) piece of fresh root ginger, finely chopped

1 teaspoon salt

10g (¼oz) shallots, finely chopped

1 tablespoon light soy sauce

1 tablespoon sesame oil

1 teaspoon soft brown sugar

24 wonton wrappers (available from Chinese or Asian grocers)

100ml (3½fl oz) Shaoxing rice wine (available from Chinese or Asian grocers)

freshly ground black pepper

1 quantity black vinegar dipping sauce (p122), to serve

Hua juan | Spring onion and chive flower rolls

These are numerous variations of the Chinese steamed rolls and buns that are frequently eaten as snacks on the street or as part of larger selection of dim sum, which is eaten in the same way as a brunch would be in the West. These flower rolls are simple to make; however, like much of Asian food, when fresh and made well they are deliciously moreish, with a great combination of flavours.

Makes 6 rolls

1 tablespoon vegetable oil

2 garlic cloves, finely chopped

1 fresh red chilli, deseeded and finely chopped

2 onions, finely chopped

1 tablespoon light soy sauce

1 tablespoon rice vinegar

8 spring onions, finely chopped

1 bunch of fresh chives, cut into 1cm (½in) lengths

2 tablespoons sesame oil

1 quantity of yeast bun dough (see p101)

salt and freshly ground black pepper

1 Heat the vegetable oil in a wok over a medium-high heat, and add the garlic and chilli. Cook for 1 minute until fragrant. Add the onion, and stir-fry for 3–4 minutes until soft. Tip in the light soy sauce and rice vinegar, and cook for a minute or two until all the liquid has been absorbed. Add the spring onion and chives. Season with salt and lots of black pepper. Stir-fry for 1 minute until the chives have wilted. Remove from the heat, and leave to cool.

2 Cut the dough in half. Roll out each half on a floured surface to form a 30cm x 10cm (12 in x 4in) rectangle. Brush one half of the dough liberally with half of the sesame oil. Spread half the onion and chive mixture over the dough. Lay the other half of dough on top of the onion mixture. Brush again with the sesame oil, then spread out the remaining onion and chive mixture on top of this.

3 Starting with one of the long sides, roll up the dough Swiss roll-style. Pinch the two ends together to stop the sesame oil running out. Lightly flatten the roll with the heel of your hand, then cut the roll into 4cm (1¾in) pieces. Press down into the middle of each piece of dough with a chopstick, parallel to the two cut ends. Pick up each piece of dough by its rounded ends, and pull until they meet underneath the roll. Pinch the ends together. This will cause the rolls to "flower" when they are steamed.

4 Line a bamboo steamer with a piece of greaseproof paper. Place the buns on the paper, allowing space for them to rise. Steam for 10–12 minutes until the tops of the buns have "flowered". Serve immediately while they are still piping hot.

Partner with
Stir-fried greens with garlic (p18–19)
Roast pork with fresh mint and peanuts (pp158–9)

Laksa lemak | Singapore coconut laksa

There are two main styles of laksa in Singapore, *Penang laksa* and *laksa lemak*, then countless variations in terms of different recipes. This is a *laksa lemak*, which is spicy with a rich coconut cream sauce. The version here is made with fish and seafood, but you can make it with chicken, or bean curd and vegetables.

Serves 6

- 400g (14oz) raw prawns, unpeeled
- 4 garlic cloves, any green inner shoot removed, chopped
- 2 teaspoons freshly ground coriander seeds
- 1 teaspoon ground turmeric
- 4 fresh red chillies, deseeded and finely chopped
- 8 shallots, finely chopped
- 1 teaspoon shrimp paste (balachan or Thai kapi)
- 2 tablespoons macadamia nuts
- 400g (14oz) rice vermicelli
- 1 small cucumber
- 2 lemongrass stalks
- 2 tablespoons vegetable oil
- 1 teaspoon salt
- 1 teaspoon sugar
- 300ml (10fl oz) coconut cream
- 250g (9oz) firm-fleshed fish such as snapper or sea bream, cleaned, deboned, and cut into 2cm (¾in) cubes
- juice of 2 limes
- handful of fresh coriander leaves
- 200g (7oz) beansprouts, trimmed and rinsed
- handful of fresh mint leaves
- freshly ground black pepper
- lime wedges, to serve

1 Bring 500ml (16fl oz) water to the boil. Add the whole prawns and cook for 2 minutes until the prawns turn pink. Remove the prawns and reserve the liquid. Peel the prawns, slit the backs open with a sharp knife, and devein. Set aside.

2 Using a mortar and pestle, grind the garlic, coriander seeds, and turmeric to make a paste. Add the chilli and shallot, then the shrimp paste and macadamia nuts, grinding all the while. Add a little water, and keep grinding until you have a smooth paste. Set aside.

3 Soak the rice vermicelli in boiling water for 2 minutes until soft; drain. Cut the cucumber into 4cm (1¾in) lengths, then cut the flesh into slices; discard the central core of seeds. Restack the slices and cut the cucumber into matchsticks. Remove the outer leaves of the lemongrass stems, then bruise the stems with back of a knife.

4 Heat the oil in a heavy pan over a medium heat, and add the reserved spice paste. Stir-fry for about 5 minutes until fragrant. Add the reserved prawn cooking liquor, lemongrass, salt, and sugar, and bring to the boil. When the water has boiled, add the coconut cream. Simmer for 8–10 minutes until the liquid starts to thicken.

5 To serve, arrange 6 deep bowls, adding some noodles to each bowl. Season the fish with black pepper; add to the simmering liquid. Poach for 3–4 minutes until cooked. Add half the lime juice and half the fresh coriander. Check the seasoning. Thirty seconds before you remove the pan from the heat, add the reserved prawns and the beansprouts. Divide the fish, prawns, and beansprouts between the bowls, and ladle over the soup. Garnish with the remaining coriander leaves, mint leaves, cucumber, and lime wedges.

Bakwan kepiting | Nonya pork, prawn, and crab ball soup

Nonya cuisine is very creative and distinctive; it is a mixture of Chinese and Malay, with Indonesian and Thai overtones. The Nonya have a taste for plenty of fresh coriander, yet less dried spices are used than in typical Malay cuisine, with coriander, cumin, and fennel seeds being the main choices.

1 Cover the shiitake mushrooms in boiling water and soak for 30 minutes. Drain the mushrooms and finely chop, reserving the mushroom liquid. Slice the asparagus spears on an angle, into 3cm (1¼in) spears. Set aside.

2 To make the meatballs, combine the mushrooms, pork mince, prawns, crab meat, chilli, spring onion, egg, and cornflour in a bowl. Season well with salt and black pepper. Take a small piece of mixture and fry it in a small frying pan. Taste the mixture, and adjust the seasoning to suit your taste.

3 To make the soup, heat the vegetable oil in a heavy pan over a medium-high heat. Fry the garlic slivers for 1–2 minutes until golden brown and crisp. Remove the garlic with a slotted spoon, and drain on kitchen paper. Pour in the chicken stock and bring to the boil, then reduce to a simmer. Add the soy sauce and reserved mushroom liquid to the stock.

4 Meanwhile, shape the pork mixture into balls about 2.5cm (1in) in diameter. Drop the balls into the simmering liquid – they will take 4–5 minutes to cook. When ready, they will float to the surface.

5 Two minutes before serving, add the asparagus spears. Taste the soup and adjust the seasoning with salt, black pepper, and a little lime juice, which will highlight the flavours. a minute before removing the soup from the heat, add the beansprouts. Ladle the soup into serving bowls, and add the poached pork balls. Garnish with the slivers of fried garlic and lots of fresh coriander.

Serves 4–6

2 dried shiitake mushrooms

8 fresh asparagus stems

250g (9oz) lean pork mince

150g (5oz) raw prawns, peeled, deveined, and finely chopped

150g (5oz) picked crab meat

2 fresh red chillies, deseeded and finely chopped

3 spring onions, finely chopped

1 egg, lightly beaten

½ teaspoon cornflour

1 tablespoon vegetable oil

3 garlic cloves, any green inner shoot removed, cut into slivers

1 litre (1¾ pints) chicken stock

2 tablespoons light soy sauce

juice of 1 lime

100g (3½oz) beansprouts, trimmed and rinsed

handful of fresh coriander leaves

salt and freshly ground black pepper

Partner with
Stir-fried beansprouts with hot red bean paste (p21)
Burmese turmeric fishcakes (pp80–1)

Sambal babi | Nonya-style spicy pork

This simple pork dish from Singapore bears all the characteristic well-balanced flavours of Nonya cuisine. Hot, sweet, salty, and sour are all represented. It works particularly well when eaten as part of a larger meal.

Serves 4

500g (1lb 2oz) lean pork

4 dried chillies

8 shallots, chopped

1 teaspoon balachan or kapi (shrimp paste)

2 tablespoons vegetable oil

3 tablespoons tamarind pulp (see p154)

1 teaspoon sugar

1 tablespoon light soy sauce

handful of fresh coriander leaves

salt and freshly ground black pepper

1 Cut the pork into slices about 1cm (½in) thick, then cut those slices into pieces 5cm (2in) long and 1cm (½in) wide. Soak the dried chillies in boiling water to soften. Remove the seeds and discard, and finely chop the flesh.

2 Using a mortar and pestle, pound the chilli, shallot, and shrimp paste to a fine paste. Heat the vegetable oil in a wok over a medium heat. Fry the paste gently for 4–5 minutes until fragrant.

3 Add the pork slices, and cook until golden brown on all sides and coated in the spice paste. Add the tamarind pulp and sugar, and season with salt and black pepper. Finally, add the light soy sauce and enough cold water to almost cover the meat. Simmer, uncovered, stirring the mixture frequently to avoid the meat sticking. When the sauce has reduced and thickened, add the coriander leaves and serve hot.

Partner with
Sardines with green chilli sambal (pp46–7)
Nonya bean curd salad (pp136–7)

Fresh and aromatic

Across the many Asian cuisines, the word "fresh" need not apply only to salads, although there is certainly a wealth of these to choose from all across this vast region – and indeed in this chapter. Fresh herbs, crisp vegetables, fresh fruits and nuts, cooling yoghurt and sauces are all used to best advantage. But there are also the other "fresh" approaches such as chilled seafood, fresh-tasting chutneys, even using fresh herbs and greens for wrapping food. And all come with that characteristic aromatic pull of spices and seasonings.

Sesame chicken salad with white pepper

There are many variations of chicken salad in Southeast Asia and China. This one originates from China's Yunnan province, near the borders of Burma, Vietnam, and Laos. Vibrantly flavoured with great textures, it bears similarities to dishes from each of these countries with its use of coriander and chillies. It can be served as a meal in itself with rice or noodles, or as part of a larger Asian meal.

Serves 4–6

6 celery sticks from the centre of the bulb

handful of fresh coriander, leaves picked (keep the stems)

4cm (1¾in) piece of fresh root ginger, finely chopped (reserve the peelings for the stock)

6 white peppercorns

3 whole skinless chicken breast fillets, 500–600 g (1 lb 2 oz–1 lb 5 oz) in total

2 garlic cloves, any green inner shoot removed, finely chopped

2 fresh green chillies, deseeded and finely chopped

4 spring onions, finely chopped

2 tablespoons light soy sauce

2 tablespoons rice wine vinegar

½ teaspoon salt

1 teaspoon sugar

1 teaspoon ground white pepper

2 tablespoons sesame oil

2 tablespoons sesame seeds

Partner with
Steamed green vegetable rolls (p105)
Tamarind fried prawns (pp154–5)

1 Bring a saucepan of water to the boil, and add 2 of the celery sticks, the coriander stems, the ginger peelings, and 6 white peppercorns. When the stock is boiling, add the chicken breasts and return the boil. Simmer for 5 minutes, using a slotted spoon to skim off any scum that rises to the surface. Cover the pan with a lid, and remove from the heat. Let stand for 20 minutes – this will result in perfectly cooked and juicy poached chicken. After 20 minutes, remove the chicken from the pan and allow to cool. (You can reserve the chicken stock to use in another dish.)

2 Cut the remaining celery into thin slices, then restack and cut into thin matchsticks. Bring a little water to the boil in a small pan, and blanch the celery for 10 seconds, then refresh under cold running water to stop the cooking. Drain and set aside.

3 To make the dressing, mix the garlic, chilli, and chopped ginger in a bowl with the spring onion, light soy sauce, rice wine vinegar, salt, sugar, and white pepper. Let stand to combine the flavours. Pull apart the poached chicken into shreds about 1cm (½in) wide and 3cm (1¼in) long. Mix the shredded chicken with the celery and sesame oil. Add the dressing, and leave to stand for 5 minutes.

4 Meanwhile, in a small frying pan over a medium heat, dry-roast the sesame seeds for 3–4 minutes until they pop and turn golden brown. Tear the coriander leaves into the chicken salad, then sprinkle over the sesame seeds. Toss together and serve.

Katsuo tataki | Chilled seared tuna with ginger

This is a simple way of transforming fresh tuna to form part of a summer Asian meal. The tuna is seared, then marinated, both methods imparting their flavours and changing the textures. This method works equally successfully with a piece of beef or a fillet of venison. The tangy dressing works brilliantly with the sweetness of the tuna.

1 Heat a heavy frying pan over a medium-high heat. Take the large piece of tuna, and cut it in half across the grain. Cut each piece in half longthways again, so that you are left with four quarter pieces that are like logs. Roll the tuna logs in the sesame seeds, and season well with salt, black pepper, and the shichimi togarashi.

2 Tear off 4 pieces of foil and have them ready by the frying pan. Grease the heated frying pan with a little oil, and sear the tuna for 20–30 seconds on one side until the sesame seeds turn golden. Carefully turn the tuna over, and sear on the other side. Remove the tuna from the pan, and place each piece onto separate pieces of foil. Tightly roll the tuna in the foil, like a Christmas cracker. Put the foil parcels in the freezer for 30 minutes. This will not only stop the cooking, but also firm up the fish's texture for slicing.

3 Meanwhile, prepare the other ingredients. Finely slice the ginger, then restack on the board and cut thinly into matchsticks. Crush the garlic with a little salt using the back of your chopping knife, to form a paste. Mix the garlic paste with the lemon juice, mirin, rice vinegar, and tamari. Transfer the dressing to a shallow dish

4 Remove the tuna from the freezer, and place in the dish with the dressing. Add half the ginger and half the spring onion. Leave for 10 minutes, turning regularly so that the dressing is absorbed into the fish. After 10 minutes, remove the tuna and place on a board. Using a sharp knife, cut into thin slices 2–3 mm (about ⅛in) thick. Each slice will be rare in the centre with a seared sesame edge. Arrange on individual plates or a large platter, and spoon over the dressing. Scatter the remaining ginger and spring onion over the top.

Serves 4

500g (1lb 2oz) fresh tuna fillet (as one large piece)

4 tablespoons sesame seeds

1 teaspoon shichimi togarashi (Japanese seven-spice) (available from Japanese grocers or Asian supermarkets)

a little vegetable oil

4cm (1¼in) piece of fresh root ginger

1 garlic clove, any green inner shoot removed, finely chopped

juice of ½ lemon

2 tablespoons mirin (Japanese rice wine)

2 tablespoons rice wine vinegar

3 tablespoons tamari (Japanese soy sauce)

4 spring onions, finely chopped

salt and freshly ground black pepper

Partner with
Marinated barbecue beef (pp52–3)
Hot and sour green papaya salad (pp144–5)

Ponzu | Citrus dipping sauce

Ponzu is a delicious sauce to serve with fresh fish and shellfish, whether it is raw, seared, or lightly cooked. The name comes from the time when there were Dutch traders in Japan. *Pon* comes from the Dutch word for "citrus", and *zu*, or *su*, the Japanese word for "vinegar". All the ingredients for this dressing are available from Asian grocers and good health food shops. It is not difficult to make, but it does need to be made at least 24 hours before you need it. Still, it keeps for a long time in the refrigerator, so you could always make a large quantity.

Makes enough for 6–8 servings

a 8 x 6cm (2½in) piece of kombu (Japanese dried kelp)

250ml (8fl oz) fresh lemon juice

250ml (8fl oz) fresh lime juice

100ml (3½fl oz) rice wine vinegar

100ml (3½fl oz) mirin (Japanese rice wine)

5 tablespoons tamari (Japanese soy sauce)

40g (1½oz) dried bonito flakes

1 Take the piece of kombu in a pair of tongs, and carefully hold it over a gas flame or under a hot grill for 10–15 seconds on each side. Put in a bowl with all the other ingredients. Cover and marinate in the refrigerator for 24 hours to allow the flavours to develop.

2 Strain the liquid into a serving bowl, and use as dipping sauce for sushi, sashimi, or fried shellfish and seafood.

Black vinegar dipping sauce Chinkiang black vinegar comes from China's north and has a complex smoky flavour; it is aged in a similar fashion to balsamic vinegar. This Chinese dipping sauce goes spectacularly well with the pot-sticker dumplings on pp106–7, but can be used whenever a vinegar dipping sauce if called for. To make, put 150ml (5fl oz) Chinkiang black vinegar, 1 teaspoon sugar, and a 3cm (1¼in piece of fresh root ginger, grated, in a small pan. Bring to the boil. Simmer for 2 minutes, then remove from the heat and add 2 finely chopped spring onions. Serve as an accompaniment.

Partner with
Prawn and chive spring rolls (pp72–3)
Sesame tempura (pp78–9)

Kung sang wa | Cured prawns with shredded lime leaves

A deliciously refreshing salad, this works well as a party entrée. It takes about 10 minutes to put together the ingredients that can be prepared beforehand and about 4 minutes to cure the prawns. It is important that the fibrous and strong-tasting ingredients are shredded to allow all the invigorating flavours to be combined in one mouthful. You could use other grilled shellfish such as crayfish, lobster, or crab instead of prawns – they will provide the same sweet richness needed for this dish.

1 Using a hot barbecue or ridged cast-iron grill pan, grill the prawns whole in their shells for 2 minutes on each side, to impart greater flavour. When cooked, peel and devein, then finely shred the meat and set aside.

2 Remove the tough outer layer of the lemongrass, and finely slice the stem. Peel the ginger and cut flesh into thin slices. Restack the slices in piles on your board, and finely shred the ginger. Cut the shallots in half through the core, then slice as finely as possible so that the slivers are held together at the core. On the back of the kaffir lime leaves there is a raised stem. Using a sharp knife, shave the stem so that the leaves are flat. Tightly roll the leaves into a cigar shape. Working the knife rhythmically, finely shred the rolled lime leaves into needle-like threads.

3 Mix the lime and orange juices with the fish sauce, and stir in the sugar to dissolve. Put the prawns in the dressing with the shredded lime leaves for 3 minutes while you pick the mint and coriander. Roll up the mint leaves and shred them in a similar way to the lime leaves. Roughly tear the coriander. Mix all the remaining ingredients with the prawns, leaving the herbs until last. Taste the perfumed mixture. The prawns and the sugar provide the sweetness; the chilli will be hot; the lime juice, lime leaves, and lemongrass are sour; and the fish sauce provides the saltiness. Adjust the seasoning to suit your taste. Serve immediately.

Serves 6

12 large unpeeled raw prawns

2 lemongrass stalks

4cm (1¾in) piece of fresh
    root ginger

4 shallots

5 tender kaffir lime leaves

2 tablespoons fresh lime juice

2 tablespoons fresh orange juice

2 tablespoons fish sauce such
    as nam pla

1 teaspoon sugar

4 sprigs of fresh mint

4 sprigs of fresh coriander

2 medium-hot fresh red chillies,
    deseeded and finely chopped

3 spring onions, finely sliced

Partner with
Seared scallops with fresh
chutney (pp16–17)
Grilled beef patties with shallots
and cumin (pp26–7)

San choy bau | Fresh lettuce cups with chicken

San choy bau roughly translates as "raw vegetable", and this name is used for this dish because of the fresh crisp lettuce that is used to wrap these warm parcels. It is a dish filled with contrasting flavours and textures. Instead of chicken, try minced pork or a combination of meats. You could also use squab or duck.

Serves 6 as a starter

500g (1lb 2 oz) skinless chicken thigh fillets

3 tablespoons Shaoxing rice wine

3 tablespoons light soy sauce

2 teaspoons sesame oil

8 dried shiitake mushrooms

150g (5oz) peeled water chestnuts

1 teaspoon sugar

1 garlic clove, any green inner shoot removed, finely chopped

4cm (1¾in) piece of fresh root ginger, finely chopped

2 fresh red chillies, deseeded and finely chopped

4 spring onions, finely chopped

vegetable oil for cooking

12 crisp Little Gem lettuce leaves

salt and freshly ground black pepper

Partner with
Grilled marinated mackerel (pp22–3)
Sichuan spicy pickled cucumber (p152)

1 Put the chicken in a food processor with 2 tablespoons of the rice wine, 1 tablespoon of the light soy sauce, and 1 teaspoon of the sesame oil. Mince together until finely chopped. Cover and refrigerate for 1–2 hours. Put the dried mushrooms in a bowl, and cover with boiling water. Let stand for 30 minutes. Drain, saving the soaking liquid and squeezing any excess liquid from the mushrooms into the bowl. Discard the stems and chop the caps. Set aside.

2 Blanch the water chestnuts in a pan of boiling water for 1 minute, then refresh in cold water. Roughly chop and set aside. Mix 60ml (2fl oz) of the mushroom soaking liquid with the remaining 1 tablespoon rice wine, 2 tablespoons light soy sauce, and 1 teaspoon sesame oil. Add the sugar and stir to dissolve. Set aside.

3 Heat a wok until very hot, add 2 tablespoons vegetable oil, and swirl it around the inside so that it coats the wok. Add the garlic, ginger, chilli, and spring onion, and stir-fry for 20 seconds. Add the chicken mixture. Stir-fry for 3–4 minutes until the chicken is browned, mashing and separating the meat so that it cooks evenly. Remove from the wok and set aside. Clean the wok and return to the heat, adding a couple of tablespoons of extra oil. Add the mushrooms and water chestnuts, and stir-fry over a high heat for 1 minute.

4 Add the combined mushroom/soy sauce liquid, and bring to the boil for 1–2 minutes. Return the chicken to the wok, and combine. Continue stir-frying until the liquid has almost evaporated. Season well with salt and black pepper. Check the seasoning. Serve the chicken mixture in a central bowl on the table accompanied by the lettuce leaves. To eat, spoon some warm mixture into the centre of a lettuce leaf, and fold the lettuce around to make a parcel.

Khayanthee thoke | Grilled aubergine salad

Burma has a unique cuisine within Asia. It takes it influences from its two enormous culinary neighbours, India and China, as well as ingredients and styles of cooking from Laos, Thailand, and across Southeast Asia. Many varieties of noodles are used in Burma as a result of the Chinese influence, and the use of cumin, coriander seeds, and turmeric, as well as lots of types of beans and lentils, comes from India. There are also numerous fermented fish and seafood products from shrimp pastes to fish sauce found in Burmese cuisine, similar to those of other parts of Southeast Asia.

Serves 4–6

75g (2⅓oz) skinless raw peanuts

2 large aubergines

1 onion

2 tablespoons vegetable oil

4 garlic cloves, any green inner shoot removed, cut into slivers

1 tablespoon sesame seeds

½ tablespoon tamarind pulp (see p154)

1 tablespoon fish sauce such as nam pla

2 fresh red chillies, deseeded and finely chopped

small handful of fresh coriander leaves, roughly chopped

popadums, to serve (optional)

Partner with
Sumatran minced duck sate (pp50–1)
Crisp peanut wafers (p65)
Malay beef rendang (pp148–9)

1 Spread the peanuts out in a single layer on a baking tray, and roast in a preheated 200°C (400°F/Gas 6) oven for 4–5 minutes until golden brown. Set aside. Grill the aubergines under an overhead grill or on a char-grill until the skin is blackened all over and the aubergines are soft. Allow them to cool, then peel off the charred skin and discard. Lightly mash the flesh with a fork, then set aside. Finely slice the onion, then soak in cold water for 10 minutes. Drain.

2 Meanwhile, heat the oil in a small saucepan over a medium-high heat and add the garlic slivers. Fry for 1–2 minutes until pale golden and crisp. Make sure that the garlic does not get too dark – otherwise it will carry on cooking and become bitter. Remove with a slotted spoon and set aside. Reserve the oil. Using a small heavy frying pan, dry-roast the sesame seeds for 1–2 minutes until they pop and turn golden brown. Remove from the heat.

3 Put the mashed aubergine and drained soaked onion in a bowl. Crush the roasted peanuts, and scatter over the vegetables with the toasted sesame seeds. Mix together the tamarind pulp, fish sauce, chopped chilli, and reserved garlic oil to make a dressing. Pour over the aubergine salad. Serve as a salad, with the coriander sprinkled over the top. Alternatively, put little mounds of the salad on broken pieces of popadum, garnish with the coriander, and serve as a snack or canapé.

Chilled soba noodles with seared salmon

Soba noodles are made from buckwheat and are high in vitamin B – very good for maintaining decent energy levels. They are delicious either hot or chilled, served more as a noodle salad. You can alter what goes with them, from vegetables to fish or meat. Fresh soba noodles are preferable, but you can use dried. Once the noodles are cooked, rinse them in plenty of cold water to wash away the sticky starch.

1 Cut the asparagus into 3cm (1¼in) pieces on an angle so that the pieces look like pen nibs. To make the dressing, combine the ginger and wasabi paste in a bowl, then mix with the remaining dressing ingredients. Set aside.

2 Heat a ridged cast-iron grill pan or griddle over a high heat (there is no need to oil the pan). Season the salmon fillets with salt and black pepper. Grill for 2 minutes on each side so that the salmon is marked with bars on the outside and rare in the centre. The fish will carry on cooking after it has come off the grill; by the time it has cooled, it will be medium-rare.

3 In the meantime, put the asparagus nibs in a bowl, and splash over a little vegetable oil. Season with salt and black pepper. Toss the asparagus in the bowl so that the seasoning sticks to the asparagus. Grill the asparagus in the cast-iron ridged grill pan until charred on each side, about 4 minutes in total. Do not overcook or it will become soggy – you want it to still have bite. At the same time, roast the sesame seeds in a dry frying pan over a low heat for a few minutes until golden brown, taking care not to scorch.

4 Bring a large pan of salted water to boil. Add the noodles and cook for 4–5 minutes until al dente. Cool in plenty of cold water, then drain in a colander. Put the cold noodles in a large bowl, and pour over the dressing, then add the chilli and spring onion. Mix together. Taste the noodles, and adjust the seasoning in the dressing to suit your taste. Flake the salmon into the noodles, and add the grilled asparagus. Lightly mix together, then scatter the sesame seeds over the top. Serve immediately.

Serves 4

1 bunch of fresh asparagus

2 salmon fillets, about 200g (7oz) each

a little vegetable oil

4 tablespoons sesame seeds

400g (14oz) soba noodles

1 fresh red chilli, deseeded and finely chopped

4 spring onions, finely sliced

salt and freshly ground black pepper

For the dressing

4cm (1¼in) piece of fresh root ginger, finely grated

2 teaspoons wasabi paste (available from Japanese or Asian grocers)

3 tablespoons light soy sauce

2 tablespoons sesame seeds

2 tablespoons rice vinegar

100ml (3½fl oz) dashi stock (see p97)

Partner with
Miso soup with seven-spice chicken (pp96–7)
Spring onion and chive flower rolls (pp110–11)

Manda uppilittathu | Rena's South Indian mango pickle

Unripe green mangoes are used in this fantastic mango pickle, as opposed to the sweeter ripe mangoes found in other versions. It is delicious when accompanying fish and vegetable dishes, with its freshness and balance of flavour and texture. If curry leaves are not available, use some fresh coriander leaves instead.

Serves 6

2 unripe green mangoes

5 shallots, finely sliced

3 large fresh green chillies, deseeded and finely chopped

1 teaspoon salt

3 tablespoons vegetable oil

½ tablespoon black mustard seeds

2 level teaspoons chilli powder

½ teaspoon ground turmeric

1 level teaspoon asafoetida powder

10 curry leaves (preferably fresh)

squeeze of lemon juice (optional)

1 Peel the mango and cut into 1cm (½in) dice. Mix the mango, shallot, and chilli together in a bowl, and sprinkle with the salt. Leave to sit for 30 minutes.

2 Heat the oil in a heavy saucepan over a medium-high heat. Add the mustard seeds, and stir for about 30 seconds until they start to pop. Add the remaining spices, the curry leaves, and any liquid that has accumulated from the salted mangoes. Heat vigorously for 2 minutes until the spices are fragrant.

3 Pour the spice mixture over the mango. Stir together, check the seasoning, and adjust the salt to taste. You will have a refreshing balance of hot, sweet, salty, and sour. If the sourness is not coming through, refresh the mango pickle with a squeeze of lemon juice. Allow the mixture to cool, then taste again to adjust the seasoning and correct the balance.

Partner with
Keralan spiced chickpea and lentil dumplings (pp56–7)
Carrot pachadi (pp162–3)

Chamandhi | Fresh coconut chutney

This is a delicious Southern Indian condiment that goes well with many dishes. It complements grilled fish or marinated chicken dishes perfectly, and you are just as likely to have it in India, Sri Lanka, or Singapore. Be warned: it won't last long, as it is so tasty it is likely to be readily devoured by guests and cook alike.

1 Using a mortar and pestle, pound the garlic and ginger to a paste. Add the salt and green chilli, and continue to pound until smooth. Add the coconut and 2 tablespoons water, and keep pounding together. (If using desiccated or shredded coconut rather than fresh, you can use 2 tablespoons of the soaking liquid to bring the coconut into a thick paste.)

2 Heat the oil in a frying pan over a medium-high heat. Add the mustard seeds, and fry for 20–30 seconds until they start to crackle and become aromatic. Add the shallot, curry leaves, and chilli flakes, and cook for 2–3 minutes until softened. Remove from the heat, and mix together with the coconut paste.

3 Finally, add the coriander leaves and lime juice, and remove the curry leaves from the chutney, as you want only their flavour. Blend well and taste. The coconut will be sweet and the chilli hot, while the seasoning and lime juice cut the potential fattiness of the coconut. There should be a good balance of all the flavours. Adjust with more salt or lime juice if necessary.

Serves 6–8

1 garlic clove, any green inner shoot removed, finely chopped

2cm (¾in) piece of fresh root ginger

½ teaspoon salt

1 fresh green chilli, deseeded and finely chopped

200g (7oz) grated fresh coconut (you could use unsweetened desiccated or shredded coconut soaked in warm water)

1 tablespoon vegetable oil

1 teaspoon brown mustard seeds

1 sprig of curry leaves (preferably fresh)

3 shallots, finely sliced

½ teaspoon dried chilli flakes

30 fresh coriander leaves

juice of 1 lime

Partner with
Isaan-style grilled chicken (pp40–1)
Gujarati aubergine fritters (pp82–3)

Crisp cabbage salad with peanuts

A deliciously crisp and refreshing salad that stimulates all the senses, this dish is visually appealing, with lots of interesting textures and well-blended flavours that wake up your taste buds and leave your mouth alive. It originates from Laos in the centre of Southeast Asia, and you will find similar dishes in Thailand, Vietnam, and Singapore.

Serves 4–6

100g (3½oz) skinless raw peanuts

1 hard white Chinese cabbage

4cm (1¼in) piece of fresh root ginger

1 tablespoon olive oil

6 shallots, finely sliced

1 garlic clove, finely chopped

2 fresh red chillies, deseeded and finely chopped

1 tablespoon soft brown sugar

juice of 2 limes

3 tablespoons light soy sauce

1 tablespoon rice vinegar

3 spring onions, finely chopped

handful of fresh mint leaves

handful of fresh coriander leaves

salt and freshly ground black pepper

Partner with
North Vietnamese fish brochettes (pp46–7)
Tamarind beef with peanuts (pp180–1)

1 Spread out the peanuts in a single layer on a roasting tray and bake in a preheated 200°C (400°F/Gas 6) oven for 4 minutes or until golden brown. Remove from the oven and leave the peanuts to cool, then roughly crush. Set aside. Remove the tough outside leaves of the cabbage and discard. Cut the cabbage in half, and remove the heart. Finely shred the leaves and put in a large bowl. Finely slice the ginger, then rearrange the slices into stacks on the board and finely shred into thin matchsticks. Set aside.

2 Heat a large frying pan over a medium-high heat. Add the olive oil and stir-fry half of the shallot for 2 minutes until it starts to caramelize. Push the shallot to one side of the pan, and add the garlic and chilli. Stir-fry for 1–2 minutes until fragrant. Add the brown sugar and half of the crushed peanuts. Allow the sugar to melt and coat the peanuts. Mix everything in the pan together, remove from the heat, and transfer to a small bowl.

3 Combine the lime juice, soy sauce, and rice vinegar. Pour over the caramelized shallot and peanut mixture. Season with salt and black pepper. Check the seasoning, and adjust if necessary. It will be hot, sweet, salty, and sour. Add 2 tablespoons water to thin the dressing – this does not really dilute the flavours; they are supposed to be quite intense.

4 Mix the shredded cabbage with the remaining shallot, the spring onion, and the ginger. Tear in the mint and coriander leaves. Dress with the warm peanut dressing and serve immediately, with the remaining crushed peanuts scattered over the top.

Taukwa goreng | Nonya bean curd salad

Variations of these crunchy vegetable salads are found in Nonya cooking throughout Singapore and Malaysia, as well as in Indonesia. You could use sesame seeds instead of nuts if you prefer. Any combination of vegetables can be used – try some lightly blanched or quickly grilled, while leaving others raw.

1 Cut the cucumber in half lengthways and remove the seeds with a teaspoon. Finely slice the cucumber flesh. Cut four large slices off the sides of the red pepper, leaving the central core of seeds on the inside. With a sharp knife, remove the white pith and membrane from the pepper slices; discard. Cut the pepper into thin slices. Top and tail the mangetout. Stack two or three of the mangetout on top of each other, and shred into thin matchsticks. Continue until all the mangetout are shredded. Set aside.

2 To make the dressing, dry-roast the nuts in a heavy pan over a medium heat until golden brown. Shake the pan occasionally, and be careful not to scorch the nuts. Remove from the heat, and allow the nuts to cool. Using a mortar and pestle, grind the ginger, chilli, and shallot to a paste. Add the roasted nuts and continue to crush, then add the palm sugar and work until smooth. Add the remaining dressing ingredients and mix together. The dressing will be sweet and hot; salty and sour.

3 Heat enough oil for deep-frying in a large heavy pan over a medium-high heat. Wipe the bean curd dry with kitchen paper, and deep-fry in the hot oil for 4–5 minutes until golden brown all over. Drain on fresh kitchen paper, and cut into ½cm (¼in) slices.

4 Bring a pan of salted water to the boil. Blanch the mangetout and beansprouts in the boiling water for 30 seconds, then quickly refresh under cold running water to stop them cooking. Mix the blanched vegetables with the cucumber and red pepper. Scatter over the fried slices of bean curd with the spring onion and coriander leaves. Spoon the roasted nut and tamarind dressing over the top, and serve the salad immediately.

Serves 4–6

1 large cucumber

1 red sweet pepper

200g (7oz) mangetout

vegetable oil for deep-frying

250g (9oz) hard bean curd

150g (5oz) beansprouts, trimmed and rinsed

2 spring onions, finely chopped

handful of fresh coriander leaves

For the dressing

4 tablespoons skinless raw peanuts or raw cashew nuts

3cm (1¼in) piece of fresh root ginger, finely chopped

2 fresh red chillies, deseeded and finely chopped

4 shallots, finely chopped

1 tablespoon palm sugar or soft brown sugar

1 tablespoon dark soy sauce

3 tablespoons tamarind pulp (see p154)

3 tablespoons warm water

salt and ground black pepper

Partner with
Curried sweetcorn fritters (pp70–1)
Sumatran aubergine sambal (pp88–9)

Keynotes | Coriander, basil, and mint

Fresh herbs are essential to good food all across the vast region of Asia. Coriander, mint, Thai basil, chives, watercress, Vietnamese mint, shiso, Asian celery, long-leaf coriander, dill, curry leaves – all are used to provide perfumed freshness in the vibrant patchwork of dishes that make up an Asian meal.

In Vietnam, many dishes are served with what is known as a "table salad". This accompanies soups, salads, spring rolls, and curries; diners then tear a selection of fresh leaves into their food. A typical table salad includes coriander leaves, mint, Thai basil, Vietnamese mint, beansprouts, and lime wedges. Turkish and Central Asian food also feature accompanying bowls of fresh herbs.

Coriander

Coriander (*Coriandrum sativum*) is said to be the most-consumed herb on the planet, spreading its tendrils across South, East, Central, and Western Asia; the Middle East; and much of East Africa and South America. Native to the Middle East, it is documented as being in China around 200 BC.

Fresh coriander heightens the flavour of other ingredients, while also moderating rich flavours with its fresh citrus taste. It is often sold with its roots intact; these are used chopped and pounded to form a base in curry pastes, sauces, and dressings, and provide an intense depth of flavour for dishes such as Thai green curry. Coriander seeds are a

Thai basil

Coriander

foundation ingredient in an Asian spice collection and have little similarity in taste to the fresh herb. They benefit hugely from dry-roasting and are used in Middle Eastern, Indian, Thai, and Malaysian dishes.

Long-leaf, or saw-leaf, coriander (*Eryngium foetidum*) has a more pronounced taste. It is best chopped finely or cooked, and is found in Vietnamese and Thai cuisine.

Mint

Coriander seeds

"Fresh coriander heightens the flavour of other ingredients, while also moderating rich flavours with its fresh citrus taste."

Coriander root

Basil

Holy basil (*Ocimum tenuiflorum*) is also called sacred basil or tulsi. An important plant in the Hindu religion, it is also used in ayurvedic medicine. Thai basil (*Ocimum basilicum*) is also known as Asian basil and licorice basil, and it has an intense lemony aniseed aroma. It works very well with spices such as cinnamon, star anise, and ginger. The common cultivar "Queen of Siam" has dark green leaves with a purple tinge, and purple stems.

Mint

Mint (*Montha* spp.) is very versatile and widely used throughout Southeast Asia, in particular Vietnam. This herb originated in Greece and from there spread widely into West and Central Asia, and down into India. There are said to be 30 different varieties. Two of the most widely used are common or garden mint with its sweet smell, and spearmint, which has a narrow leaf with a serrated edge and a distinctive fresh flavour.

Vietnamese mint

Vietnamese mint (*Polygonum odoratum*), or *rau ram*, has many names, including Vietnamese coriander, Cambodian mint, and hot mint, yet it is not actually a true mint. Its dark green spear-shaped leaves flecked with purple have a strong, pungent, and peppery acidic taste – a few leaves go a long way. It is used in Singaporean and Malaysian soups, as well as Thai salads and Vietnamese summer rolls and table salads.

Asian salad with pea shoots and sprouts

This salad is fresh and vibrant, and uses sprouts and shoots, which are full of vitamins and minerals. It calls for fresh turmeric, which is available from Chinese grocers or Thai and Asian food stores. When peeled and used fresh in thin slices, turmeric provides a fantastic peppery bite to dishes such as salads and soups. It is worth trying to get hold of some if you have never seen or used it before.

Serves 4–6

3cm (1¼in) piece of fresh turmeric

2 limes

100g (3½oz) pea shoots, trimmed and rinsed

100g (3½oz) mung bean sprouts, trimmed and rinsed

100g (3½oz) mustard cress shoots, trimmed and rinsed

100g (3½oz) alfalfa sprouts, trimmed and rinsed

30 fresh mint leaves

handful of fresh coriander leaves

2 handfuls of mixed peppery leaves including rocket, watercress, and mizuna

5cm (2in) piece of fresh root ginger

For the dressing

3 tablespoons extra virgin olive oil

juice of 1 lemon

½ teaspoon ground turmeric (only if fresh turmeric is not being used in the salad)

1 fresh red chilli, deseeded and finely chopped

1 teaspoon runny honey

salt and freshly ground black pepper

1 As turmeric is a strong natural dye, you will need to wear a pair of rubber gloves while preparing to avoid staining your fingers bright orange. Peel the turmeric. Discard the peel and, using a vegetable peeler, shave the turmeric root into slivers. Put in a bowl and cover with fresh water until ready to use.

2 Using a thin sharp knife (it could be serrated), cut the skin and pith off the limes. When all the flesh is exposed, hold the fruit in one hand and cut each segment on the inside of the membrane. Keep the lime segments in a bowl to catch any juices. Peel the ginger and slice finely, then stack together and cut into fine matchsticks.

3 Put all the shoots and sprouts in a large bowl. Add the herbs and mixed leaves. Combine all the ingredients for the dressing. If you are using fresh turmeric, drain first, then add to the dressing; if not, simply add the ground turmeric along with the other dressing ingredients. (The honey in the dressing softens some of the acidity and the salad's peppery elements.) Add the ginger, lime segments, and any extra lime juice. Season well with salt and black pepper.

4 Pour the dressing over the sprouts and leaves, and toss gently to a form a vibrant, vitamin-packed combination of textures and flavours that will give your taste buds a real workout. Serve straight away, before the acidity of the dressing starts to wilt the leaves.

Monlar oo thoke | Pickled daikon salad with fried garlic

Sesame and peanuts are grown in the hot central area of Burma and feature together in many of the dishes from this region. This simple refreshing salad with its crisp textures and an intense blend of hot, sweet, salty, and sour flavours is characteristic of much of Southeast Asian cooking. It can be eaten as a starter, but also works well as an accompaniment to other dishes.

Serves 4–6

3 tablespoons rice vinegar

1 teaspoon salt

1 teaspoon sugar

1 fresh red chilli, deseeded and finely chopped

1 large daikon (mooli or Japanese radish), about 450g (1lb) peeled

2 tablespoons skinless raw peanuts

1 tablespoon sesame seeds

3 tablespoons vegetable oil

6 garlic cloves, any green inner shoot removed, finely sliced

3 spring onions, finely sliced

handful of fresh coriander leaves

1 tablespoon fish sauce such as nam pla

1 tablespoon garlic oil

1 Put the vinegar, salt, and sugar in a large bowl. Stir together to dissolve the granules. Add chilli to the vinegar solution. Using a vegetable peeler, peel the daikon into thin ribbons. Toss in with the vinegar solution, and marinate in the refrigerator for 15 minutes.

2 Preheat the oven to 200°C (400°F/Gas 6). Spread the peanuts on a baking tray or sheet. Roast in the oven for 4–5 minutes until golden brown, then roughly crush. Set aside. Roast the sesame seeds in a dry frying pan over a medium-high heat for 2–3 minutes until they pop and are golden – be careful not to scorch them. Remove from the heat and set aside.

3 Heat the vegetable oil in a small frying pan over a medium heat, and fry the sliced garlic for 1–2 minutes until crisp and golden brown. Using a slotted spoon, remove the garlic from the pan, and drain on kitchen paper. Reserve the oil for dressing the salad (or use bought garlic-infused oil, if you wish).

4 When ready to serve, remove the pickled daikon from the refrigerator, and tip off any excess liquid. Add the spring onion, toasted sesame seeds, and crushed peanuts. Tear the coriander into the salad. (It is important not to tear the coriander leaves until you are actually adding them to the salad, as they will otherwise lose flavour and vitality.) Add half of the fried garlic. Combine the fish sauce with 1 tablespoon of the garlic oil, and use to dress the salad. Garnish with the remaining coriander leaves and garlic, and serve immediately.

Partner with
Malay fried noodles (p20)
Roast pork with fresh mint and peanuts (p159)

Cho go chu jang | Sashimi of sea bream with hot dressing

Korea's position on a peninsula, surrounded by sea, means that there is a bounty of fish and seafood in the Korean diet. Sashimi is a common way of eating fresh fish such as sea bream or the highly acclaimed kingfish. The style of eating this freshest of fish is different, however, to the Japanese method of the same name. Korean food exists as medicine as well as sustenance, and so an ongoing balance of ingredients is sought to achieve the right harmony of the body and the taste buds. The seasoning of red chilli gives the fresh raw fish extra vibrancy.

1 It is essential that the fish is very fresh. Get your fishmonger to pin-bone the fish and skin it. Alternatively, do this yourself. To skin the fish, dip your finger and thumb into some salt, so that you can get a good grip of the tail end of the fish – the salt will work as an abrasive. Using a thin sharp knife, insert the blade down into the flesh near the tail end. Work your knife gently along so that the blade is horizontal to the skin, pointing away from you. Increase the tension in your thumb and finger holding the tail. Run the knife in long, smooth strokes from left to right away from you, running along and separating the skin from the flesh. At the same time, pull the skin towards you at the same speed as the knife, so that piece of fish is being worked into the path of knife in your other hand.

2 Finely slice the fish across the grain into thin complete slices. If not using immediately, store in the refrigerator until needed. With the back of a knife, work the garlic, pinch of salt, and sugar on a chopping board, to make a smooth pulp. Mix the crushed garlic with the kochujang in a bowl. Add the sesame oil, light soy sauce, and lemon juice, and mix together.

3 When ready to serve, gently lay the slices of fish on a serving platter. Season with black pepper, and scatter with spring onion. Pour over the spicy sesame dressing and serve. There will be a fantastic combination of hot, salty, and sour flavours, which combine with the sweetness of the fresh fish.

Serves 4

500g (1lb 2 oz) sea bream, sea bass, or kingfish (choose the freshest fish possible)

1 garlic clove, any green inner shoot removed, finely chopped

pinch of salt

1 teaspoon sugar

2 teaspoons Sunchang kochujang (Korean hot red bean paste)

3 tablespoons sesame oil

2 tablespoons light soy sauce

juice of 1 lemon

3 spring onions, finely sliced

freshly ground black pepper

Partner with
Laotian spice-pickled spring onions (pp168–9)
Sichuan peppered beef (pp170–1)

Yam som tam | Hot and sour green papaya salad

Whenever I am travelling in Thailand and Southeast Asia, this is the first thing that I want to eat. It epitomizes everything that is good about Thai food. You have all the elements of hot, sweet, salty, and sour present in every mouthful. The textures also combine to give your mouth a workout – there are crisp, crunchy, chewy, and soft all together. The colours are fresh, and so all your senses are stimulated. In the hot tropical humidity of Southern Thailand, this is the ultimate refreshment. Unripe papaya is hard and green-skinned; you should be able to find it in Asian grocers.

Serves 4

- 1 large green unripe papaya (available in Thai and Asian grocers)
- 4 tablespoons skinless raw peanuts
- 3 garlic cloves, any green inner shoot removed, finely chopped
- 4 hot fresh bird's-eye chillies, deseeded and finely chopped
- pinch of salt
- 2 tablespoons small dried shrimp
- 1 tablespoon palm sugar or soft brown sugar
- 8 cherry tomatoes, cut into quarters
- juice of 2 limes
- 2 tablespoons fish sauce such as nam pla

1 Peel the skin off the papaya and discard. Continue to peel the flesh into strips. Stack the strips on a chopping board, then use a knife to chop them into thin matchsticks. Dry-roast the peanuts in a heavy pan over a medium-high heat for 3–4 minutes until golden brown. Shake the pan frequently, and be careful not to scorch the peanuts. Remove from the heat and allow to cool.

2 Using a large mortar and pestle, pound the garlic, chilli, and a pinch of salt to a paste. Add the dried shrimp and sugar, and continue to pound to break the prawns down (as they are hard). Add the tomato and gently crush – be careful that it does not splash too much. Lastly, add the lime juice and fish sauce to make a dressing.

3 Pour the dressing over the green papaya. Using the mortar and pestle, lightly crush the roasted peanuts so that they are broken up. Scatter the crushed peanuts over the papaya. Toss the salad together, and serve immediately for a true taste sensation.

Partner with
Stir-fried beef with chilli and onion relish (p33)
Spiced prawn cakes on sticks of lemongrass (pp34–5)

Tangy and refreshing

When many people think of Asian food, they think of heat, as in chillies. Yet there is another aspect of Asian food that should not be neglected, and that is those dishes that are almost an explosion of tang and flavour – a firework display for your taste buds. Tamarind, citrus, lemongrass, and lime leaves play a role in this, as well as other key ingredients in the Asian spice collection such as Sichuan pepper and turmeric. Chutneys, pickles, dipping sauces, and vegetable dips also demonstrate a concentration of flavour that is refreshing and enlivening.

Rendang daging | Malay beef rendang

A dish clearly showing the mix of cultures that influence Malaysian food, this dry beef curry has virtual cult status in Malaysia. The beef is cooked very slowly so that the juices are absorbed and evaporate, leaving the meat meltingly soft – a cooking method that is also found in India. The flavourings of lime leaves, lemongrass, and galangal, however, mark rendang's foundations in Southeast Asia.

Serves 4–6

2 tablespoons vegetable oil

750g (1lb 10oz) beef shin, trimmed and cut into 2cm (¾in) cubes

1.5 litres (2¾ pints) coconut cream

1 tablespoon tamarind pulp

1 teaspoon ground turmeric

5 kaffir lime leaves

a little freshly squeezed lime juice

salt and freshly ground black pepper

For the spice paste

8 fresh red chillies, deseeded and finely chopped

10 shallots, finely chopped

4 garlic cloves, finely chopped

4 lemongrass stems, tougher outer layer removed, finely chopped

4cm (1¾in) piece of fresh root ginger, finely chopped

2 teaspoons soft brown sugar

Partner with
Indonesian fried rice (p32)
Sumatran aubergine sambal (pp88–9)
Singapore coconut laksa (p112)

1 Put all the spice paste ingredients in a food processor, and blend to a smooth paste. You may need to add a little of the coconut cream to keep the blade turning.

2 Heat a heavy pan over a medium-high heat. Add the oil, and fry the spice paste for 4–5 minutes until fragrant. Season the beef pieces with salt and black pepper, and add to the spice paste, coating all the pieces for a further 2 minutes. Add the coconut cream, tamarind pulp, turmeric, and whole lime leaves. Bring the mixture to the boil, then reduce the heat to low and simmer very gently.

3 Stir the meat every 10 minutes to avoid it sticking, and simmer until the liquid has almost dried up and the meat is tender, at least 1½ hours. Add a little water only if the liquid dries up before the meat is tender. Continue to cook the beef until the sauce has become a thick coating paste and the curry is almost dry. Be patient: this method of slow-cooking only enhances the final flavour.

4 Taste the rich sauce. It will be hot and slightly sour, with an underlying sweetness from the coconut cream. Adjust the seasoning with salt and a little lime juice to balance the flavours. Although rendang is a dish that takes quite a long time to cook, it is not complicated and definitely worth the wait. Serve as part of larger meal with rice and other accompanying dishes such as relishes, sambals, vegetable dishes, and noodles.

Batu sambol | Sri Lankan smoky aubergine dip

A similar method is used to make this dip as is found in the Middle Eastern *baba ghanoush*, where the aubergines are grilled whole over a flame. This cooks and softens the aubergines inside and imparts a smoky taste from the skin being charred on the outside. The overall flavour of the dip is enriched with ground almonds.

1 Heat an overhead grill or a cast-iron ridged grill pan until very hot. Place the aubergines under or on the grill, and blacken all over, allowing 3–4 minutes on each side. Grill for a total of 12–15 minutes until the skin is charred and the flesh inside softened and cooked. Remove from the heat and allow to cool.

2 Heat a heavy pan over a medium-high heat. Add the 2 tablespoons olive oil, and sweat the onion for 5–7 minutes. Push the onion to one side of the pan, then add the ginger, garlic, and chilli. Fry the aromatics in the oil for 2 minutes until fragrant, then stir into the onion mixture. Reduce the heat to low.

3 Cut the softened aubergine in half lengthways, and scoop out the flesh and seeds. Discard the skin, and chop the flesh. Add the tomato purée, paprika, cinnamon, and cumin to the onion mixture, and cook over a low heat for 4–5 minutes until fragrant. Mix in the chopped aubergine flesh, and cook for a further 2 minutes to combine all the flavours. Stir in the ground almonds and chopped coriander. Season well with salt and black pepper.

4 Transfer the mixture to a blender or food processor, and purée until smooth. While the motor is running, gradually add the extra 75ml (2½fl oz) olive oil in a thin, constant stream, as you would when making a mayonnaise. Pour in the lime juice and mix together. Check the seasoning. The dip will be hot from the chilli and the spices, salty and smoky from the seasoning and grilling, sweet from the onion and the cooked aubergine, and sharpened by the lime juice. Add more salt, lime juice, or fresh chilli if required, so that all the flavours are balanced. Serve with plenty of hot fresh bread as the start of a meal or use as a relish or condiment as part of a larger meal.

Serves 4–6

2 large aubergines

2 tablespoons olive oil plus 75ml (2½fl oz) extra

1 onion, finely chopped

3cm (1¼in) piece of fresh root ginger, finely chopped

2 garlic cloves, finely chopped

1 fresh red chilli, deseeded and finely chopped

1 teaspoon tomato purée

½ teaspoon paprika

1 teaspoon ground cinnamon

1 teaspoon ground cumin

1 tablespoon ground almonds

1 small bunch of fresh coriander, leaves picked and chopped

juice of 1 lime

salt and freshly ground black pepper

Partner with
Seared scallops with fresh chutney (pp16–17)
Fried puffed potato bread (pp62–3)

Sichuan spicy pickled cucumber

Pickled vegetables are hugely popular in China and indeed throughout Asia. This particular recipe is intensely flavoured and is usually eaten as a snack or at the beginning of the meal. Many of the hot pickles that are sold use chilli or chilli oil to obtain the heat; this one uses some Sichuan pepper as well, which imparts a slight numbing sensation to the tongue.

Serves 6 as a snack

300g (10oz) cucumbers

½ teaspoon salt

5cm (2in) piece of fresh root ginger

1 fresh red chilli, deseeded and finely chopped

3 tablespoons sesame oil

½ teaspoon Sichuan pepper

½ teaspoon crushed dried chilli flakes

2 tablespoons rice vinegar

1 tablespoon sugar

1 Cut the cucumbers in half lengthways, and remove the central core of seeds. Cut the cucumber flesh into 6cm x 2cm (2½in x ¾in) batons. Put the cucumber in a bowl, and sprinkle over the salt. Mix together and leave for 30 minutes.

2 Pour off any water in the bowl that has accumulated from the cucumber. Lightly rinse the cucumber under cold running water, then pat dry with kitchen paper. Thinly slice the ginger, then finely shred. Put the cucumber in a clean bowl with the ginger and chopped red chilli.

3 Heat a saucepan over a medium-high heat, and add the sesame oil and Sichuan pepper. Cook for 15–30 seconds until fragrant. Add the crushed chilli flakes and mix together, then pour the liquid over the cucumber. Toss together and leave to cool.

4 When the cucumbers are cool, mix the vinegar with the sugar until dissolved. Add the vinegar mixture to the cucumber, and toss together to coat. Leave for any time from 2–6 hours – the longer you leave it, the softer the cucumber will be. Serve as a snack or to accompany grilled meat dishes as part of a larger meal.

Partner with
Sesame chicken salad with white pepper (pp118–19)
Sichuan peppered beef (pp170–1)

Nuoc dau phung | Vietnamese peanut dipping sauce

From Indonesia to Vietnam, countless versions of peanut sauce can be found across Southeast Asia. This one is very light, rather than heavy and cloying, enabling you to taste all the ingredients. It works spectacularly well with the happy crêpes on pp86–7, but also makes a great condiment for other seafood and grilled and barbecue meat.

1 Roast the peanuts for 3–4 minutes until golden brown. Roughly chop 1 tablespoon of the nuts and crush the rest. Using the back of a knife, crush the garlic with a little salt on a board.

2 Heat the oil in a heavy pan over a medium-high heat, and fry the garlic, chilli, and ginger for 3–4 minutes until fragrant. Add the crushed peanuts (reserving the chopped ones to use later), reduce the heat, and cook for a further 3–4 minutes.

3 Add the water or chicken stock, along with the sugar and all the other liquids except the lime juice, and bring to the boil. Reduce the heat, and simmer for 12–15 minutes until the oil from the peanuts has risen to the surface. Remove from the heat and allow to cool, then add the lime juice and chopped peanuts. Transfer to a serving bowl for dipping.

Serves 6

3 tablespoons skinless raw peanuts

1 garlic clove

a little salt

1 tablespoon vegetable oil

1 small fresh bird's-eye chilli, deseeded and very finely chopped

2cm (1in) piece of fresh root ginger, finely grated

100ml (3½fl oz) water or chicken stock if available

4 tablespoons coconut cream

2 teaspoons sugar

1 tablespoon fish sauce such as nuoc nam

1 tablespoon hoisin sauce

juice of 1 lime

Partner with
Minced pork balls with garlic and pepper (pp38–9)
Happy crêpes (pp86–7)
Tamarind fried prawns (pp154–5)

Asam udang | Tamarind fried prawns

With this simple and very delicious recipe, you enjoy a blend of the four major tastes – hot, sweet, salty, and sour – in one mouthful. You could use the marinade for fish or other shellfish because both of the latter are sweet and complemented well by the flavours here. Chicken or pork could also be used.

Serves 4–6

600g (1lb 5oz) unpeeled
 raw prawns

2 tablespoons tamarind pulp
 (see right)

1 tablespoon light soy sauce

½ teaspoon sugar

1 teaspoon crushed black pepper

½ teaspoon crushed dried chilli

2 tablespoons vegetable oil

salt

1 Slit the back of the raw prawns, peel, and devein using a sharp knife. Mix all the marinade ingredients except the salt in a bowl. Add the prawns, cover, and leave to marinate in the refrigerator for at least 1 hour, turning the prawns two or three times to ensure that they are fully coated in the marinade.

2 Season the prawns with salt. Heat the oil in pan over a medium-high heat, and fry the prawns until they are dark brown on both sides. These can be served as a starter with some cucumber slices or as part of a large meal with a number of components.

Preparing tamarind Tamarind is a seed pod that has brown skin the colour of cinnamon. The flesh is sticky and meaty like a date, but has stringy membranes and hard stones. It is available in a number of different forms: as raw pods, as a rough cake of the pressed meat, or bought processed as tamarind pulp in a jar, which is by far the easiest form with which to work. It is also available as a concentrate, which I think is too strong – it is very black and too overpowering in its concentration. If you are using the rough cake of pressed tamarind meat, place the meat in a large bowl and cover with hot water. Leave to soften for about an hour, then massage the flesh away from the stones and the stringy membranes, discarding both the stones and membranes. Add some more water to the tamarind paste to form a tamarind pulp. This pulp will keep in an airtight glass jar in the refrigerator for 1–2 weeks.

Partner with
Malay fried noodles (p20)
Grilled beef patties with
shallots and cumin (pp26–7)
Spring onion pancakes (pp60–1)

Keynotes | Preserved fish products

The salty element of Asian cooking comes in many forms – fermented soya bean products, such as soy sauce, tempeh, and bean paste, for instance. The other main area where salt is found is in dried and fermented fish products. The intense tropical humidity that exists across much of China and Southeast Asia, combined with a lack of proper refrigeration, means that fish and seafood spoil very easily if not eaten straight away. In the past, the only way to preserve much of it was to dry it in the sun, salt it, or allow it ferment. These preservation methods are widely used across Southern China, Southeast Asia, Malaysia, and Indonesia. Salting and drying change the flavours from subtle to intense and powerful. As a result, dried and preserved seafood are seen more as condiments or flavourings, and used more sparingly than if fresh.

Dried seafood can be steamed, fried, or grilled, then used in combination with other, fresher ingredients. It includes fish, large, medium and tiny; scallops; abalone; squid and cuttlefish; jellyfish; oysters; and shrimp and prawns.

Dried shrimp

These staple dried ingredients are widely used. In Thailand, Singapore, and Vietnam, stalls sell scores of different varieties. Every shade of orange and pink, ranging minutely in size, is represented, in open sacks like grain or rice. The smell of them on such a large scale is intensely pungent; they are best used in small portions. In China, dried shrimp appear in soups and rice dishes, and stuffed with minced pork in wonton dumplings. In Thailand, they are used in noodle dishes and pounded into salads such as the amazing *yam som tam*, hot and sour green papaya salads that originated from what is now Laos and have cult status all over Southeast Asia. In Malaysia, dried shrimp are crushed and added to spicy sambals. They can be steamed or soaked, lightly toasted, or simply crushed with garlic and chilli using a mortar and pestle. When crushed, they lose their intense pungency, instead becoming aromatic and flavourful. Dried shrimp are best kept in airtight containers and can be bought from any Chinese or Asian grocer.

Shrimp paste

There are various forms of this pungent fermented paste across Southeast Asia. In Thailand it is called *kapi*, which is made by putting small shrimp into jars of salt and leaving them to ferment. The shrimp almost digest themselves as their digestive enzymes break down. In Malaysia, another version is made called *balachan*, a paste of pulverized shrimp and salt that is spread on a mat to dry in the sun. This paste is packed into bricks, then sold in smaller blocks or slices. Both are very pungent. When shrimp paste is wrapped in banana leaves or foil, and baked or dry-roasted for 5–10 minutes, the pungency disappears and the paste becomes aromatic. Blended with other flavours in curry pastes, marinades, dressings, and sambals, it imparts an intense depth of flavour with salty and savoury characteristics, rather than fishy ones. *Sambal balachan* is a Malaysian paste of chillies, shrimp paste, lime leaves, and lime juice.

Fish sauce

Known as *nuoc nam* in Vietnam and *nam pla* in Thailand, fish sauce is essential to the cooking of Vietnam, Thailand, Burma, Cambodia, Laos, and the Philippines in the same way that soy sauce is to Chinese and Japanese cuisine. The aroma is stronger than the taste, and takes a bit of getting used to. Again, on its own it is strong and pungent; however, when combined with complementary elements such as lime juice, chilli, and fresh herbs, it is transformed. When cooked, it loses its fishy taste and adds depth of flavour instead.

Fish sauce is made by packing small anchovy-like fish in barrels of brine, which are left to ferment in the sun for a few months. The resulting brown liquid is highly nutritious. In Vietnam, there is a saying: "Without good fish sauce, food can never taste good, regardless of how talented the chef." This archetypal sauce is used to season food, as well being one of the main ingredients of the typical dipping sauces found in Southeast Asian cuisine. The best fish sauce comes from an island called Phu Quoc off the coast of Vietnam; the first run-off liquid is light amber and fragrant, and is best used for dipping sauces so that it is not cooked – rather like the finest extra virgin olive oil.

Shrimp paste

Fish sauce

Dried shrimp

"Salting and drying change the flavours from subtle to intense and powerful. As a result, dried and preserved seafood are seen more as condiments or flavourings."

Bun bi suon | Roast pork with fresh mint and peanuts

Two of the thrilling things about Southeast Asian food are the combination of different flavours in balance and the varying textures found in a single dish. This dish from Vietnam is no exception. The soft, chewy, and crisp textures of the pork, cucumber, and beansprouts all seem to be exaggerated when put alongside crunchy peanuts.

1 Preheat the oven to 200°C (400°F/Gas 6). Place an ovenproof dish over a medium-high heat. Season the pork with salt and black pepper. When the dish is hot, add a little oil and the piece of pork. Seal the meat for 2 minutes on each side until it is browned. Transfer to the oven, and roast for 20 minutes or until cooked. Remove from the oven and leave to cool.

2 While the pork is cooking, prepare the other ingredients. Spread the peanuts in a single layer on a baking tray, and roast in the oven for 4–5 minutes until golden. Remove from the oven and allow the peanuts to cool, then roughly crush using a mortar and pestle. Cut the cucumber into 5cm (2in) lengths. Cut thin vertical slices of the cucumber flesh, leaving the block of seeds in the centre untouched. Discard the seeds. Rearrange the ribbons of cucumber into stacks, then cut into thin matchsticks. Cut the shallots in half and remove the tough core. Finely slice the shallot into wafer-thin slices. The spice-pickled spring onions can be made in advance (see pp168–9).

3 To make the dressing, combine the chilli, lime juice, and fish sauce in a small bowl. Add the sugar, and stir until dissolved. Remove the pork from the roasting tray, and transfer to a board for slicing. Pour some of the dressing into the roast pork pan, and use a wooden spoon to deglaze the pan – to pick up all the good bits and juices left by the roasting. Tip back into the rest of the dressing.

4 Slice the pork and mix with the other salad ingredients (minus the peanuts and pickled spring onions). Pour over the dressing and toss together gently. Scatter over the peanuts, and serve with the spice-pickled spring onions on the side.

Serves 4–6

750g (1lb 10oz) pork tenderloin

vegetable oil for cooking

100g (3½oz) skinless raw peanuts or cashew nuts

1 cucumber

4 shallots

500g (1lb 2oz) beansprouts, trimmed and rinsed

handful of fresh mint leaves

1 quantity Laotian Spice-pickled Spring Onions (see pp168–9)

salt and freshly ground black pepper

For the dressing

2 fresh red chillies, deseeded and finely chopped

juice of 2 limes

2 tablespoons fish sauce such as nuoc nam

1 teaspoon sugar

Partner with
Prawn and chive spring rolls (pp72–3)
Fried beansprouts and clams (pp94–5)

Chutni zardolu | Spicy apricot chutney

Ripe stone fruit are used in this delicious spicy chutney hailing from Afghanistan, to preserve the fruit for the winter months. You can use apricots, peaches, nectarines, or plums, or a combination of these. It can also be made with ripe tomatoes if you like. Adjust the chilli and spice content to suit your taste. And remember that it is very easy to make a large quantity of this if you wish.

Makes 2 x 450g (1lb) jars

1.5kg (3lb 3oz) ripe apricots

250ml (8fl oz) white wine vinegar

2 tablespoons sugar

1 tablespoon salt

1 tablespoon vegetable oil

1 tablespoon coriander seeds, roughly crushed

2 garlic cloves, any green inner shoot removed, finely chopped

2 hot fresh green chillies, deseeded and finely chopped

4cm (1¾in) piece of fresh root ginger, finely chopped

1 cinnamon stick

1 Preheat the oven to 200°C (400°F/Gas 6). Put the apricots in a high-sided roasting tray. Bake in the oven for about 20 minutes until softened but not watery. Remove from the oven, and leave until cool enough to handle. Methodically work from one end of the pan to the other, removing the stone from each apricot. Transfer the flesh to a board and chop with a large knife. Reserve the juices in the pan.

2 Bring the vinegar to the boil with the sugar and salt, and simmer for 5 minutes. Using a separate pan, heat the oil over a medium-high heat, and add the crushed coriander seeds, garlic, chilli, ginger, and cinnamon stick. Cook for 2 minutes until fragrant. Add the reserved apricot juices, and simmer until reduced and syrupy.

3 Remove the vinegar mixture from the heat, and combine with the spicy syrup and the chopped apricot flesh. Mix together. Check and adjust the seasoning to suit your taste. The mixture will be hot from the chilli, and sweet, salty, and sour from the vinegar.

4 If bottling, pour into sterilized glass jars with tight-fitting lids. Seal the jars while the chutney is still hot so that the resulting steam creates a vacuum – this helps the chutney to keep better and prevents spoiling. Regardless of whether you are bottling or not, allow 24 hours before using, so that the flavours combine and mellow.

Partner with
Garlic and coriander naan (p49)
Gujarati aubergine fritters (pp82–3)

Pachadi | Carrot pachadi

A superb creation from South India comprising a great combination of flavours and textures, *pachadi* is often served with warm *dosai* and other traditional flat breads. It can be made in advance and served either warm or at room temperature. *Pachadi* also works well as part of a large Asian meal.

1 Combine the grated carrot, shallot, and chilli in a bowl, and add the salt. Mix thoroughly and set aside. Using a mortar and pestle, crush together the cumin seeds, cardamom pods, and half the mustard seeds. Discard the husks from the cardamom. Add the coconut, and pound to a rough paste.

2 Heat the oil in a large heavy pan over a medium-high heat, and fry the remaining mustard seeds for 20–30 seconds until they pop. Add the coconut mixture and fry for 2 minutes, stirring to prevent it catching. Next, add the carrot mixture. Stir-fry for another 1–2 minutes, tossing the mixture all the time.

3 Transfer to a bowl and allow to cool. Once cooled, add the yoghurt and lemon juice, and mix together. Taste the mixture, and season well with salt and black pepper, and a little extra red chilli to suit your taste. You will get a great combination of hot from the chilli, sweet from the carrot, sour from the lemon, and salty from the seasoning. Serve as individual bites in mini popadums, or alternatively pile into a large bowl and serve with flat breads such as *dosai* or garilc and coriander naan (see p49).

Serves 4–6

4 carrots, grated

4 shallots, finely sliced

1 fresh red chilli, deseeded and finely chopped

½ teaspoon salt

1 teaspoon cumin seeds

2 green cardamom pods

2 teaspoons brown mustard seeds

150g (5oz) desiccated coconut

1 tablespoon oil

3 tablespoons Greek-style yoghurt

juice of 1 lemon

salt and freshly ground black pepper

mini popadums, to serve

Partner with
Keralan chickpea and lentil dumplings (pp56–7)
Potato with turmeric and mustard seeds (pp174–5)

Kimch'i | Korean hot pickled cabbage

Kimch'i is an ancient method of preserving vegetables that has become a Korean staple. There are hundreds of different types, many of them featuring lots of garlic and chilli. It can be preserved for a long time and provides vital vitamins and minerals that are otherwise missing in the Korean winter diet. A great condiment that can be eaten with rich grilled and roasted meats, or as part of soups or a stir-fry, kimch'i is not difficult to make, but the process does extend over a couple of days.

Serves 6–8

1 long Chinese cabbage (napa cabbage)

100g (3½oz) coarse salt

1 teaspoon sugar

2½ teaspoons chilli powder

1 daikon (mooli or Japanese radish, cut into 4cm (1¾in) julienne

3 spring onions, cut into 4cm (1¾in) julienne

4 garlic cloves, finely chopped

4cm (1¾in) piece of fresh root ginger, finely chopped

1 tablespoon salted anchovies, finely chopped (optional)

1 Trim the root end of the cabbage, but do not cut or separate the leaves. Put about 85g (3oz) of the salt into a large bowl, and add 1 litre (1¾ pints) water. Stir to dissolve the salt. Add the cabbage to the bowl, bending it so that it fits and is submerged. Add a little extra water if necessary so that the cabbage is covered. Place a plate over the top, and weight down so that the cabbage is covered in the salted water. Leave at room temperature for 12 hours until the cabbage has softened.

2 Mix the sugar with the chilli powder and remaining salt. Combine with the daikon and other remaining ingredients, including the anchovy if using.

3 Sterilize a large sealable bell jar or similar in boiling water. Drain the cabbage and rinse well under cold running water. Squeeze the cabbage dry of excess water. Put the cabbage in a bowl, and gently separate the leaves, pushing spoonfuls of the spicy daikon mixture between each leaf to fill the gaps. Press the filled cabbage into the bell jar, pushing down to remove any pockets of air, then seal the jar tightly.

4 The jar of cabbage now needs to be left out of the refrigerator in a warm place (25°C/78°F) for 24 hours, to allow the cabbage to ferment. At the end of this time, transfer to the refrigerator and use as required. This spicy fermented condiment is chopped before serving and eaten cold. Serve with rich grilled or roasted meats such as bulgogi (see pp52–3).

Partner with
Stir-fried beansprouts with hot red bean paste (p21)
Marinated barbecue beef (pp52–3)

Imam bayildi | Spiced stuffed aubergine

The name of this very famous dish, with its many variations, translates as the "Imam fainted". There are two versions as to why he did. The first is that he collapsed in rapturous delight when his wife made the dish for him. The second version says that he fainted when he discovered how much of his precious olive oil had been used.

1 Preheat the oven to 200°C (400°F/Gas 6). Score the tomatoes with a sharp knife. Blanch in boiling water for 10 seconds, then refresh in cold water. Remove the skin, then cut the tomatoes in half and remove the seeds. Cut the flesh into a fine dice. Set aside.

2 Heat some of the oil in a large heavy pan. Fry the diced aubergine in small batches for 3–4 minutes until golden brown on all sides, then drain on kitchen paper. Cook in small batches so that the oil remains hot and the aubergines fry, rather than stew.

3 Put the garlic and spices in the same pan used for the aubergine; fry for about 2 minutes until fragrant. Add the onion, reduce the heat, and sweat for 4 minutes until softened. Add the currants and remove from the heat. Stir in the fried diced aubergine and diced tomato. Sprinkle over the parsley and mix together. Season well with salt and black pepper.

4 Trim the caps from the whole aubergines. Peel off 1cm (½in) strips of peel with a very sharp knife, leaving alternate stripes of peel and bare flesh. Cut a long, deep slit down the centre of each aubergine – not all the way through. Use a spoon to push open the slit, and stuff the pocket with the spiced aubergine mixture.

5 Pack the aubergines tightly into a baking dish so that they are side by side. Combine the passata with the sugar, lemon juice, remaining olive oil, and some salt. Pour over the aubergines. Spoon any leftover filling into the gaps around the dish. Cover the dish with foil, and bake in the oven for 45–60 minutes until the aubergine has softened and the sauce has reduced. Serve at room temperature with yoghurt and lots of fresh bread.

Serves 4–6

150ml (5fl oz) olive oil

4 whole aubergines (preferably the small elongated variety, available at Arab and Middle Eastern grocers)

250ml (8fl oz) passata

1 teaspoon sugar

juice of 1 lemon

Greek-style yoghurt, to serve

For the filling

4 ripe tomatoes

2 aubergines, cut into 1cm (½in) dice

4 garlic cloves, finely chopped

1 tablespoon ground cumin

1 tablespoon ground coriander

½ teaspoon cayenne pepper

2 onions, finely diced

100g (3½oz) currants

1 bunch of fresh flat-leaf parsley, leaves picked and chopped

salt and freshly ground black pepper

Partner with
Potato and cauliflower pakoras (pp66–7)
Spicy lamb-stuffed pancakes (p74)

Laotian spice-pickled spring onions

Laos is sandwiched between Thailand and Vietnam, and uses the same principles of balancing flavour as its neighbours. Its cuisine is a blend of hot, sweet, salty, and sour, and leans to the spicier, robust, and fragrant end of the spectrum. Many favourite Southeast Asian dishes have actually originated from Laos, such as the hot and sour green papaya salad which is called *yam som tam* in Thailand and is available in variations across this region. I have had variations of these deliciously addictive pickled spring onions in Vietnam as well. Make plenty of these because, once you have a taste for them, there will be no holding back.

Serves 4

3 bunches of spring onions

2 small dried chillies, crushed

1 tablespoon coriander seeds

100ml (3½fl oz) rice vinegar

juice of 1 lime

1 teaspoon salt

2 teaspoons sugar

1 fresh red chilli, deseeded and finely chopped

2 bay leaves

4 star anise

1 Trim the spring onions and, from the white end, cut into 2cm (¾in) lengths. Only cut the white and pale part of the spring onions, which are the firmest bits. When the stem starts to become too dark a green and less solid, stop slicing and set the rest of the spring onion aside (these green lengths can be used for another dish). Using a mortar and pestle, or a spice grinder, crush the dried chilli and coriander seeds.

2 Combine all the ingredients except the spring onion in a small saucepan. Bring the mixture to the boil, then simmer over a medium heat for 2 minutes. Remove from the heat, and add the spring onion. Let stand for 3 minutes. Remove the spring onion from the hot vinegar using a slotted spoon, and put in a bowl. Do not overcook the spring onion, as it will become too soft and fall apart.

3 Allow the vinegar mixture to cool completely. When cold, pour back over the spring onion. These simple and delicious pickled spring onions should still be quite firm and have a great balance between sweet, hot, salty, and sour. They can be eaten as a snack or as an accompaniment to grilled meat dishes or crispy salads with beansprouts and roasted peanuts.

Partner with
Crisp cabbage salad with peanuts (pp134–5)
Roast pork with fresh mint and peanuts (pp158–9)

Hei jiao niu rou | Sichuan peppered beef

Either beef or venison could be used for this dish. The use of pepper when cooking meat is a long-established flavour combination that works very well. Although the pepper is hot and spicy, it also has a chemical reaction with anything sweet or rich such as the fillet of beef in this recipe. Cooking a steak with salt and pepper will mean that the meat is sweater than if you cooked it without that seasoning. The pepper draws out the sweetness in the same way that salt draws out liquid.

1 Heat enough oil for deep-frying in a wok or high-sided frying pan over a high heat. Using a mortar and pestle, crush the black and Sichuan peppercorns together. Put the cubes of meat in a bowl, and add 1 tablespoon water and the rice wine. Season with the ½ teaspoon salt and some black pepper. Massage the meat with both hands for about 1 minute until the meat absorbs the liquid.

2 Quickly deep-fry the beef in two batches, cooking each batch for 40 seconds. Drain the cubes of meat on kitchen paper, and set aside. Tip all but 1 teaspoon of the oil into a metal bowl, and leave to cool. Reheat the wok and stir-fry the garlic for 30 seconds, then add the crushed black peppercorns and Sichuan pepper. Stir-fry for 10 seconds, then add the beef, oyster sauce, soy sauce, and sesame oil. Stir-fry for a few seconds more so that all the beef is coated in sauce and the crushed pepper.

3 Take a cube of beef and a little shredded lettuce, and wrap in a length of sliced cucumber. Repeat the process until all the beef has been used. Serve immediately. The lettuce and cucumber act as cooling foils to the spiciness of the meat.

Serves 4–6 as part of larger meal

vegetable oil for deep-frying

2 teaspoons black peppercorns

1 teaspoon Sichuan peppercorns

400g (14oz) beef fillet, trimmed and cut into 2.5cm (1in) cubes

2 tablespoon rice wine

½ teaspoon salt

3 garlic cloves, finely chopped

2 teaspoons oyster sauce

2 teaspoons light soy sauce

1 teaspoon sesame oil

freshly ground black pepper

shredded lettuce, to serve

cucumber, sliced thinly lengthways, to serve

Partner with
Stir-fried greens with garlic (pp18–19)
Steamed prawn wontons (pp98–9)

Joojeh kabab | Lemon and saffron chicken kebabs

In this Iranian recipe, a blindingly simple but delicious marinade transforms chicken into something really spectacular. There is nothing complicated about the dish; the key is in marinating the chicken for as long as possible, preferably overnight. Ideally, you should use a small baby chicken or poussin, which is very tender. Alternatively, use halved chicken pieces with the skin on or, as here, skinless chicken breast fillet.

Serves 4

4 skinless chicken breast fillets, cut into strips or large cubes, or 4 baby chickens or poussin, or halved chicken pieces such as thighs, breasts, and drumsticks

2 onions

juice of 2 lemons

½ teaspoon cayenne pepper or paprika

1 teaspoon saffron threads

salt and freshly ground black pepper

chopped fresh flat-leaf parsley, to garnish

lemon wedges, to serve

Partner with
Turkish courgette fritters (p64)
Spiced stuffed aubergine (p165)
Saffron ice cream (pp210–11)

1 If using small baby chicken or poussin, take one and turn it over so that the back is exposed. Using a pair of kitchen scissors, cut down one side of the backbone from end to end. Repeat with the other side, removing the bone section, which is almost triangular in shape. With the backbone removed, place the chicken on a chopping board breast-side up. Using the side of a large kitchen knife, press down on the bird with the knife, flattening the flesh and the remaining bones at the back. This is what is referred when you are asked to "spatchcock" something. Repeat with all the birds.

2 For each bird, take a skewer and pin the thigh to the wing section on each side. If you are using chicken pieces or breast fillet, simply thread the meat onto several skewers to form kebabs. (Bamboo skewers will need to be soaked for 30 minutes or so first.)

3 Place the skewered chicken in a large flat dish. Grate the onion onto the flesh. Pour the lemon juice over the top, and scatter with plenty of black pepper and the cayenne or paprika. Rub the marinade into any crevices, and leave to marinate in the refrigerator for at least 3 hours, or preferably overnight, turning regularly.

4 When ready to cook, heat a barbecue and allow the coals to whiten. If you are using a ridged cast-iron grill pan, heat until very hot. Remove the chicken from the marinade, and place the skewers on the grill. Add the saffron to the marinade, and season well with salt. Gently grill the chicken, basting constantly with the saffron marinade. Continue to turn and baste until the meat is tender. Serve scattered with chopped parsley and lemon wedges.

Aloo chaat | Potato with turmeric and mustard seeds

Savoury potatoes such as this are often served as a filling for *dosai* or other breads, such as *puri* (see pp62–3) or paratha. Singapore has a large Indian population, and the dishes from this community are popular throughout the region. You will find a similar dish in Sri Lanka and India, as well as Pakistan and Central Asian countries. This makes a tasty accompaniment to a larger meal consisting of numerous dishes.

Serves 4–6

500g (1lb 2oz) waxy potatoes
(you could use a firm floury
variety such as Maris Piper)

2 teaspoons coriander seeds

2 tablespoons oil

1 teaspoon brown mustard seeds

1 onion, finely chopped

½ teaspoon ground turmeric

½ teaspoon red chilli powder

4 spring onions, finely sliced

juice of 1 lemon

handful of fresh coriander leaves

salt and freshly ground
black pepper

1 Boil the potatoes whole in plenty of salted water until cooked, but still firm to the point of a knife. Peel using a sharp knife, and cut into 1cm (½in) cubes. Set aside.

2 Using a mortar and pestle, roughly crush the coriander seeds. Heat the oil in a heavy pan over a medium-high heat. Add the mustard seeds and crushed coriander seeds. Fry for 30 seconds or so until the mustard seeds start to pop. Add the onion, and reduce the heat. Gently sauté the onion for 5 minutes until soft and a pale golden colour. Add the turmeric and chilli powder, and stir to combine. Season well with salt and black pepper.

3 Add the diced potato, and fry for a couple of minutes until it is hot and all the flavours have combined. Add the spring onion and lemon juice, and finish with the coriander leaves. Add more salt or dried chilli to suit your taste.

Partner with
Spicy green beans with
chilli (pp30–1)
Fried puffed potato
bread (pp62–3)

Keynotes | **Citrus and lemongrass**

The fresh clean citrus zing that makes your tongue tingle is a vital characteristic of Asian food. It can be as simple as a wedge of lemon or lime with some grilled prawns or much more complex, in the form of lemongrass and lime leaves with the addition of tamarind. Whatever form, the sour citrus notes are essential not because they have a nice flavour (although this is true), but because when combined with the other strong flavours in Asian cuisine they bring everything into balance. In Thai cooking this is called *rot chart*, or "correct taste". The opposite of hot is sweet because the acid in chilli is soluble in sugar, not water. This is why, when you have something that is too hot or spicy, you should cool it with yoghurt, cucumber, or honey, or something sweet. The opposite of salty is sour. When these four elements are combined, there is a perfect balance of flavour and the food is delicious.

The role of citrus

Citrus cuts through the fattiness and richness of foods such as roast pork or coconut cream. It also refreshes and enlivens any dish, forming contrasts between ingredients. A squeeze of citrus at the end of cooking works much like a highlighter pen on a page of writing. It draws attention to certain elements and helps them to stand out – it makes other ingredients work harder.

Kaffir lime leaves

Kaffir limes

Lemongrass

Lime juice

Lemons and limes (*Citrus* spp.) are probably the most widely used citrus around the world. Lemons originated in India and were brought to Europe by the Romans in the 1st century AD. These fruits have

"Citrus notes are essential not because they have a nice flavour (although this is true), but because when combined with the other strong flavours in Asian cuisine they bring everything into balance."

been used as food and medicine in Asia for thousands of years. They both work as the perfect natural flavour enhancer. If something you are cooking is over-seasoned and too salty, simply add a squeeze of lemon or lime juice to readjust the balance and counter the saltiness.

Both the zest and the juice can be used in many different styles of dish. The zest provides all the vibrancy, but with none of the acid. When you are zesting citrus, it is important that you zest only the thin skin that contains all the citrus oils, not the bitter thick white pith. Also, to maximize the amount of juice that you can get out of a tough lemon or lime, roll the fruit firmly under your hand on a board with your weight on top. This breaks down the fibres inside, resulting in lots more juice.

Lemongrass

Lemongrass (*Cymbopogon citratus*) is mostly used in Thai and Vietnamese cuisine, and some Malay and Indonesian food. This highly perfumed reed-like plant is native to Southeast Asia and has an amazing lemony perfume, but without the acidity of citrus.

Fresh lime

Lemongrass is used in a number of ways. The tough stalk is pounded and bruised to release the aromas, then cooked whole to impart a huge burst of flavour as in *tom yam* (hot and sour soup).

Alternatively, the tough outer layers of the stalk are removed, leaving the more tender stem inside. This is finely chopped into thin rounds and added to salads and garnishes. It must be cut very finely; if too thick, it would be a bit like chewing a stick.

In Southeast Asia, the flavourful stems are also used as skewers, to impart their unique aroma. Lemongrass also features as one of the main ingredients of Thai curry pastes and marinades.

Kaffir limes

Kaffir limes (*Citrus hystrix*) are often called fragrant limes or makrut limes, and look quite unusual compared to regular limes. The skin is dark green and very knobbly. Both skin and the fragrance of the juice are very intense, reminiscent of a citric essence or the most expensive type of perfume. There is much less juice than with ordinary limes, but a little goes a long way. Kaffir lime zest can be grated into curry pastes, marinades, and herb dressings. The zest can also be frozen for later use. If kaffir lime is not available, simply use more ordinary lime. The kaffir lime tree also produces a fragrant dark green leaf that is common in the Southeast Asian larder. Used whole in soups and curries, or finely shredded as a garnish and marinade ingredient, the leaves are best kept in a sealed bag in the freezer – this holds their colour and prevents them from drying out. The leaves defrost in seconds and can then be finely chopped or shredded, or used whole to flavour sauces.

Kai ge | Fried aubergine with toasted sesame seeds

With a Korean meal, lots of small dishes come to the table at the same time. Some are hot; some are served cold. Others are vegetables or condiments with varying textures and tastes. One dish may be highly spiced, while another may have no spice or be lightly pickled. This delicious aubergine dish with sesame seeds is great eaten hot or cold, and could be made into a more substantial salad.

Serves 6

4 aubergines

3 tablespoons salt

5cm (2in) piece of ginger, cut into thin matchsticks

2 tablespoons light soy sauce

1 tablespoon sesame oil

1 tablespoon rice vinegar

olive oil for frying

3 garlic cloves, finely chopped

100g (3½oz) sesame seeds

juice of 1 lime

salt and freshly ground black pepper

Partner with
Marinated barbecue beef (pp52–3)
Steamed green vegetable rolls (p105)

1 Cut the aubergines into 2cm (¾in) cubes and put in a large colander. Sprinkle the 3 tablespoons salt over the aubergine, and mix together so that they are all covered. Leave to drain for 30 minutes. This process removes the bitterness from the vegetable, as well as excess water. Meanwhile, prepare the other ingredients. Finely slice the ginger, then restack the pieces and cut into a fine needle shred. Mix together the light soy, sesame oil, and rice vinegar.

2 After 30 minutes, rinse the aubergine under cold water to wash off the bitter liquid and the salt. Shake off any excess water while it is in the colander, then pat dry with kitchen paper.

3 I prefer olive oil to fry vegetables with, but you can use any vegetable oil. Heat a heavy pan over a medium-high heat, and add 3–4 tablespoons olive oil. In three or four batches, shallow-fry the aubergine until it is mid golden brown on all sides. Fry in small batches so that the temperature of the oil does not drop – this ensures that the aubergines fry, rather than stew. When cooked, remove from the pan with a slotted spoon, and drain the on kitchen paper. Add a little more olive oil between each batch if necessary.

4 When all the aubergines are cooked, fry the garlic and sesame seeds until golden brown. Return the aubergine to the pan together with the ginger, and mix together. Add the soy and sesame liquid, and stir through. Season well with salt and black pepper, and pour over the lime juice. Taste the aubergine, and adjust the seasoning to suit your taste. It should be sweet, salty, sour, and well seasoned. Eat hot or cold as an accompaniment to grilled or roasted meats, or alternatively make into a more substantial salad.

Tamatar chatni | Tomato chutney with green chilli

Smooth and spicy, this tomato relish works very well with freshly grilled fish or marinated chicken, or could be served alongside vegetable dishes. It is simple to make, and it is also very easy to increase the quantities of the ingredients to make a larger batch. This way you can keep some in sterilized jars in the refrigerator for use whenever you fancy, or you might like to give it away as gifts. You will not be able to part with too much of this, however, as you will want to keep it for yourself.

1 Cut the tomatoes in half. Using a cheese grater, grate the flesh into a bowl, holding the skin side in the palm of your hand. This is a quick way of getting a tomato pulp, and the skin stays in your hand to be discarded when you are finished. Set aside.

2 Heat the oil in a heavy pan over a medium-high heat. Fry the garlic for 2 minutes until fragrant, then add the onion and reduce the heat. Cook down slowly for 5 minutes until softened. Add the ground cumin and turmeric to the pan, and cook for 1 minute to allow the flavours to combine before adding the green chilli. Stir together, then tip in the tomato pulp. Season with the salt and some black pepper, and simmer slowly for 5 minutes until everything is well blended and the tomato liquid has cooked off.

3 Transfer the mixture to a blender or food processor, add the lemon juice, and purée until smooth. Taste and adjust the seasoning. If the tomatoes are a bit too sour, sprinkle in the brown sugar and stir through. The chutney will be hot from the chilli, sweet from the onion (and sugar), and salty and sour from the lemon juice.

Makes 2 x 450g (1lb) jars

8 tomatoes

1 tablespoon vegetable oil

6 garlic cloves, any green inner shoot removed, finely chopped

2 onions, finely chopped

1 teaspoon ground cumin

1 teaspoon ground turmeric

2 fresh green chillies, deseeded and finely chopped

½ teaspoon salt

juice of 1 lemon

1 teaspoon soft brown sugar (optional)

freshly ground black pepper

Partner with
Isaan-style grilled chicken (pp40–1)
Rice flour pancakes (p81)
Carrot pachadi (pp162–3)

Trai me thit bo | Tamarind beef with peanuts

I tasted this very effective beef dish as a guest at someone's house while making a TV series in Vietnam about this country's vibrant food. It is strikingly different because of the tamarind caramel and the semi-pickled onions. At first glance, there may seem to be a lot of sugar, but it is well balanced by the tamarind and vinegar. Use a tender cut of meat that can be cooked very quickly. You could also use chicken or pork.

Serves 4–6

400g (14oz) beef rump, cut into thin slices

2 teaspoons fish sauce such as nuoc nam

2 teaspoons light soy sauce

2 tablespoons tamarind pulp (see p154)

2 tablespoons vegetable oil

2 garlic cloves, minced

4 teaspoons white sugar

100g (3½oz) skinless raw peanuts

1 onion, finely sliced

2 tablespoons rice wine vinegar

small handful of fresh coriander leaves, roughly chopped

small handful of fresh mint leaves, roughly chopped

small handful of rocket or mustard leaves or watercress, or a mixture of peppery, zesty leaves, roughly chopped

salt and freshly ground black pepper

Partner with
Sumatran minced duck sate (pp50–1)
Burmese spiced split pea fritters (pp90–1)

1 Put the beef in a glass or ceramic dish or bowl. Season well with black pepper. Combine the fish sauce and soy sauce, pour over the beef, and marinate in the refrigerator for 30 minutes.

2 Dissolve the tamarind pulp in 75ml (2½fl oz) water. Heat half of the oil in a heavy pan over a medium-high heat. Fry the garlic for about 2 minutes until golden brown, then add the tamarind liquid and half of the sugar. Reduce the heat to medium, and continue to cook until the liquid reduces to a thick syrup the consistency of honey.

3 Roast the peanuts in a dry frying pan until golden brown. Be careful not to scorch them. Remove from the heat and allow to cool, then roughly chop and set aside. Put the onion in a bowl with the vinegar and remaining sugar. Season with salt, and mix together to semi-pickle the onion. Heat the remaining oil in a clean pan. Stir-fry the slices of marinated beef in small batches until golden brown, then set aside.

4 Quickly toss together the coriander, mint, and other leaves, and arrange in a layer over the bottom of a flat serving dish. Spoon the semi-pickled onion over the top, adding all the juices. Place the beef on top of the onion. Alternatively, arrange in individual small bowls or glasses. Pour over the caramelized tamarind syrup, garnish with peanuts, and serve.

Sugar and spice

Sweet treats in Asia range from fresh tropical fruit and thirst-quenching drinks, through to more elaborate cakes, pastries, and puddings featuring spices and nuts. Often, the perfect end to a meal of hot, spicy dishes is simply a fresh fruit salad or a cooling citrus or coconut dessert. There are other times, however, when a rich saffron ice cream or perhaps crisply battered pears drenched in scented honey syrup is the order of the day. And there is no need to limit your enjoyment to mealtimes. Pastries and cakes make great snacks at any time.

Woon ma praw orn | Citrus and young coconut jelly

This is a striking-looking jelly because it has two layers: one which is clear with the citrus zest suspended in it, while the other is made from coconut cream with suspended strips of coconut in it. For visual appeal, make it in small clear shot glasses; alternatively, make it in a flat tray, then cut into squares or diamond shapes.

Serves 8

250ml (8fl oz) coconut water (the liquid from the packet of frozen young coconut)

15g (½oz) powdered agar agar

pinch of salt

250g (9oz) white caster sugar

85–100g (3–3½oz) young coconut meat, shredded (available from the freezer section of Chinese, Thai, and Asian grocers)

500ml (16fl oz) coconut cream

grated zest of 1 orange

grated zest of 1 lemon

fresh jasmine flowers (optional) (see note)

1 Combine the young coconut liquid with 750ml (1¼ pints) extra water, and pour into a small saucepan. Stir in the agar agar. Bring the liquid to a simmer, and continue to simmer for 10 minutes. Add a pinch of salt and the sugar, and stir to dissolve. Remove from the heat. Mix the shredded young coconut meat with the coconut cream. Mix in half of the reduced sugar water. Warm in a separate pan, but do not allow to boil.

2 Add the orange and lemon zest to the second half of the sugar water. Leave to cool. The orange colour of the zest will leach into the water. (Lime zest and lemon zest could be added instead, to alter the colour and flavour.) Taste the two liquids. The salt will bring out the flavour of the coconut.

3 The two liquids will start to set as they cool, much more quickly than if gelatine had been used. Quickly but carefully pour the coconut cream and meat into clean moulds, shot glasses or a flat tray. Leave a space at the top for the clear orange jelly.

4 When the white coconut jelly is starting to set and will hold the other liquid, carefully pour the clear orange jelly over the top. Leave to set in the refrigerator for 1–2 hours before turning out. The orange jelly could be poured into the mould first, to reverse the colours. Be extra careful if you choose to do this because the white coconut jelly is heavier. Serve with tropical Asian fruits, if liked.

Note The jasmine flowers can be warmed in the sugar syrup and set in the citrus jelly, for decoration. If agar agar is not available, you could use gelatine. Do not set the jelly so hard that it is rubbery.

Partner with
North Vietnamese fish brochettes (pp46–7)
Mangosteen, lychee, and mango salad (p208)

Yogurtlu samfistigi kek | Yoghurt and pistachio cake

Variations of yoghurt and nut cake abound throughout the Levant and Middle East, and have been made for centuries. This particular one originates from Turkey. When paired with some bright coloured fruits such as pomegranate or roasted quince, it takes on a regal elegance. This would not have been out of place at a palace feast in the once-opulent Persian empire. This cake takes an hour to bake if you choose to make it whole, but minutes to put together. Small individual cakes will obviously take less time. You can bake the large cake in advance, even the night before if you wish, but individual cakes should be made fresh.

1 Preheat the oven to 180°C (350°F/Gas 4). Lightly grease and flour a tin for individual cakes (such as a muffin or friand tin) or a round 20–25cm (8–10in) springform cake tin.

2 Grind the pistachio nuts and walnuts in a food processor (you can leave some in slightly bigger chunks to add some texture to the cake). Sift the flour with the bicarbonate of soda, baking powder, and salt. Add the orange and lemon zest.

3 In another bowl, beat the egg yolks with half of the sugar until pale and mousse-like. Mix in the yoghurt and olive oil, then fold in the ground nuts and flour mixture. Beat the egg whites with the cream of tartar until they form soft peaks. Tip the remaining sugar into the egg whites, and continue to beat until they are stiff (the whites should be glossy and hold their shape).

4 Gently fold the egg whites into the batter (be careful not to knock too much air out of the mixture). Pour into the prepared tins or tin. Bake in the centre of the oven for 20 minutes if baking small individual cakes or 55 minutes if using a large pan. Remove the cakes or cake from the oven, and sit on a wire rack. Allow to cool in the tin, then turn out and dust with icing sugar before serving with fresh pomegranate, if you like.

Serves 6

125g (4½oz) skinless pistachio nuts

40g (1¼oz) walnuts

150g (5oz) plain flour

½ teaspoon bicarbonate of soda

½ teaspoon baking powder

½ teaspoon salt

grated zest of 1 orange

grated zest of 1 lemon

6 eggs, separated

225g (8oz) sugar

150g (5oz) Greek-style yoghurt

125ml (4fl oz) olive oil

½ teaspoon cream of tartar

icing sugar, to dust

fresh pomegranate seeds, to serve (optional)

Partner with
Spicy lamb-stuffed pancakes (p74)
Afghan caramelized quince compote (p191)

Keynotes | **Nuts and seeds**

Asian cuisine abounds with dishes featuring nuts and seeds. Nuts have a large percentage of oil and are also high in protein, so they are very important in the Asian diet. Ground nuts and sesame seeds are

> "Ground nuts and sesame seeds are used in condiments, sauces, soups, salads, and sambals not only for the texture and body that they provide, but also for their nutritional value."

used in condiments, sauces, soups, salads, and sambals not only for the texture and body that they provide, but also for their nutritional value.

Sesame seeds

Sesame seeds (*Sesamum indicum*) are available in both white and black varieties. In cultivation since 3000 BC, they originated in India and soon travelled to Assyria in Central Asia, as well as to East Africa, and have been used in China for at least 2,000 years. Sesame seeds are used widely in Middle Eastern, Southeast Asian, and Chinese kitchens. They are crushed in pastes and made into oils, as well as eaten raw and toasted. In North and Western China, a sesame paste similar in some ways to the Middle Eastern tahini is made with toasted seeds.

Sesame oil can vary from pale golden to dark rich brown, depending on whether the sesame seeds are toasted or the oils blended. The blended toasted oil gives a wonderful aromatic quality to marinades and dressings, but needs to be used sparingly so that it does not overpower the food.

An introduced favourite

The cashew nut is actually the fruit of a small tree, *Anacardium occidentale*, which is a member of the Anacardiaceae family, along with the mango, pistachio, poison ivy, and poison oak. Cashew nuts are native to northeastern Brazil. The Portuguese introduced cashews to the west coast of India and East Africa in the 16th century, shortly after they first found it in 1578. After its planting in India, more-refined methods for removing the caustic shell oil were developed, and India is given credit for developing the modern nut industry.

Pistachio nuts

Pistacia vera are native to Western Asia and Asia Minor, from Syria to the Caucasus and Afghanistan. Archaeological evidence in Turkey indicates the nuts were being used for food as early as 7,000 BC. Pistachio nuts cannot tolerate excessive dampness and humidity, so, although they are used extensively in Western Asia, and parts of Central Asia, Pakistan, and India, they are not used at all in Eastern and Southeast Asia. Pistachios are prized for their ornamental colour and flavour. They are used both raw and roasted, and can be salted or used in desserts such as baklava and similar pastries common throughout the Middle East, Western Asia, and what was once Persia. The bright green colour bewitches the eye, creating jewelled dishes the like of which has been used to impress royalty for millennia.

Cashew nuts are now a high-yielding cash crop grown in many countries. Vietnam grows 28 per cent of the world's crop, and India still grows 25 per cent. On India's west and south coast, cashews are used in pilafs, desserts, and curries, as well as chutneys. Ground cashew nuts are used to thicken and enrich curries that would traditionally have been served for banquets and sumptuous occasions. Cashew nuts are also used in Chinese and Malaysian cooking, but are usually left whole.

More than a snack food

Although peanuts (*Arachis hypogaea*) are considered to be nuts culinary-wise, botanically they belong to the legume family Fabaceae, which includes lentils, soya beans, and peas. Peanuts originated in South America, where archaeological evidence shows that they were cultivated as far back as prehistoric times; they have been found in Peruvian tombs dating back to 1500 BC. The Portuguese transported peanuts first to Africa, then to the Malay archipelago, from where they quickly spread throughout Asia. In Asia, peanuts are much more than a snack food. They are nutritious and contain valuable vitamin E, niacin, folacin, calcium, phosphorus, magnesium, zinc, iron, riboflavin, thiamine, and potassium.

Cashew nuts

Peanuts

Sesame seeds

Pistachio nuts

Sheer berenj | Persian rice pudding with cardamom

At its height the vast Persian empire spread from Baghdad and eastern Iraq, over the whole of Iran, through Afghanistan and parts of Pakistan to the east and in the other direction as far as the eastern half of modern-day Turkey. The empire's exquisite food, sumptuous with fruits, nuts, and spices, was revered for more than a thousand years.

Serves 4–6

250g (9oz) short-grain rice

1 litre (1¾ pints) milk

85g (3oz) caster sugar

1 tablespoon honey

½ teaspoon ground cardamom

1 egg yolk

60ml (2fl oz) double cream

2 tablespoons skinless pistachio nuts, roughly crushed or chopped

1 Put the rice in a saucepan, and cover with cold water. Bring to the boil and simmer, uncovered, for 4 minutes. Drain the rice and return to the pan with the milk, sugar, and honey. Add the cardamom. Bring to the boil, then simmer over a low heat for 15 minutes, stirring regularly to avoid sticking, until the milk is absorbed.

2 Beat the egg yolk with the cream and until pale and mousse-like. Add the pistachio nuts, reserving some to garnish. When the rice is cooked, stir the cream mixture into the rice pudding. Serve hot, warm, or cold. It is made even more special when served with poached or roasted fruits, such as quince, apricots, or rhubarb.

Compote e behi (Afghan caramelized quince compote) Quinces develop a rose-pink tinge and wonderful scent when cooked. If not available, use pears, apricots, or peaches. Using a mortar and pestle, crush 2 green cardamom pods and 4 cloves until fine. Pass through a fine sieve to remove any woody bits. Peel, quarter, and core 4 quinces, then put in a pan. Mix the sieved spices with 100g (3½oz) sugar, and scatter over the fruit. Add 150ml (5fl oz) water, and bring to the boil over a medium-high heat. Reduce the heat and simmer for 50 minutes until the quinces are soft. Remove the fruit from the syrup with a slotted spoon. Simmer the liquid for about 5 minutes until reduced by half. Add the juice of ½ lemon and taste. If necessary, add a little extra sugar. Heat an overhead grill until hot. Place the poached quince quarters on a baking tray, and spoon over the scented syrup. Place under the hot grill for 3–4 minutes until the tops are golden and caramelized. Pour over the excess syrup, and serve with clotted cream, crème fraîche, or ice cream. This compote works well with Yoghurt and Pistachio Cake (pp186–7). Serves 4–6.

Partner with
Keralan spiced chickpea and lentil dumplings (pp56–7)
Lemon and saffron chicken kebabs (pp172–2)

Miwa naurozee | Afghan new year compote

Miwa means "fruit" and *nauroz* means the "new year", reflecting the roots of this compote of dried fruit and nuts that is traditionally prepared to celebrate the advent of spring, which is considered the "new year" in Afghanistan. It can be made with any combination of fruits or nuts, and is great eaten with cream or cream-based desserts.

1 Wash the apricots and other dried fruits, then put in a large bowl and cover with plenty of cold water. Leave the fruits to soak for 2 days to ensure maximum plumpness.

2 Put all the nuts in a separate bowl, and cover with boiling water. Leave to soak until the water has cooled, then rub the skin from the nuts. Removing the skins from walnuts is quite a fiddly job, and you will need a small knife to get under the skins. Despite being a bit time-consuming, it is definitely worth the effort because the nuts are so delicious. When finished, discard the water you have used to soak the nuts. Set the nuts aside.

3 When the fruits have been soaked for 2 days, drain the liquid into a small pan. Add the honey, orange juice, and the spices. (It is much better if you freshly grind your own spices; if you don't, just make sure you use the freshest ones you can.) Bring to the boil, and simmer until the juices start to turn syrupy. Combine the fruits and nuts, then mix in the spiced syrup. Serve warm or chilled.

Serves 6

110g (4oz) dried apricots

50g (1¾oz) light-coloured raisins

110g (4oz) dark seedless raisins

50g (1¾oz) sour cherries

50g (1¾oz) walnuts

50g (1¾oz) almonds

50g (1¾oz) pistachio nuts

2 tablespoons honey

juice of 1 orange

1 cinnamon stick

½ teaspoon freshly grated nutmeg

½ teaspoon ground allspice

½ teaspoon ground cloves

Partner with
Turkish courgette fritters (p64)
Lamb pilaf with saffron and nuts (p104)

Sharbat | Sour cherry sherbet

A *sharbat*, or sherbet, is a refreshing fruit syrup cordial that can be kept refrigerated until needed. On a hot day, pour it over crushed ice or dilute with mineral water for a thirst-quenching drink. You can also mix the base with some yoghurt or cream, or pour it over ice cream or fresh fruit. Vary the fruits used to make the sherbet, from dried or semi-dried fruit, to strawberries and other berries, or ripe stone fruit.

Serves 6

100g (3½oz) dried sour cherries

50g (1¾oz) dried or semi-dried cranberries

50g (1¾oz) semi-dried figs, chopped

grated zest and juice of 1 orange

1 cinnamon stick

3 bay leaves

2 tablespoons clear honey

pinch of salt

400ml (14fl oz) boiling water

1 Put the dried fruit in a metal bowl with the orange juice and zest, cinnamon, bay leaves, and honey. Pour over the boiling water. Cover and leave to stand for 40 minutes or until the fruit has absorbed as much of the liquid as possible.

2 Remove the fruit with a slotted spoon. Pour the liquid into a small pan, add a pinch of salt, and simmer over a medium heat for 6–7 minutes until the liquid has reduced by half and has started to become syrupy. (The salt helps to replace lost minerals in the body, as well as bringing out the flavours of the fruits and spices.)

3 Pour the syrup back over the fruit and use straight away. Alternatively use the fruit for one dish, maybe a dessert, and save the syrup to make a refreshing sherbet drink.

Tamarind sharbat Tamarind is used here to make a refreshing *sharbat* syrup, or cordial. Put a rough cake of 500g (1lb 2oz) pressed tamarind meat in a large bowl. Cover with 1 litre (1¾ pints) hot water. Leave to soften overnight, then massage the flesh away from the stones and stringy membranes. Rub the pulp through a fine sieve, squashing it with a wooden spoon. Sieve the pulp again, back into the soaking liquid. Strain through a clean muslin cloth into a pan. Add 400g (14oz) sugar. Bring to the boil, stirring slowly to dissolve the sugar. Simmer gently until the syrup thickens. Allow to cool, then pour into clean, dry bottles and seal tightly. The high sugar content means that the syrup will keep stored in the refrigerator. (Increase the amount of sugar if this syrup is too sour for your taste.) It makes a very refreshing drink when diluted to taste with ice-cold water.

Partner with
Grilled beef patties with shallots and cumin (pp26–7)
Sumatran minced duck sate (pp50–1)

Pineapple with caramelized chilli

Chilli with fruit is a delicious combination of flavours because the sweetness counters the heat, then is lifted by the acidity. This dish goes one step further by caramelizing the sugar and dried chilli, imparting a smoky flavour to this simple dish without cooking the pineapple. You can use this method for other fruits as well.

1 Peel the pineapple and cut in half lengthways. Cut each half into half-moon slices. Using a mortar and pestle, crush the sugar and dried chilli so that you are left with small fragments of sugar and crushed chilli. Do not crush the sugar to complete dust.

2 Scatter the chilli sugar over the pineapple, then light a chef's blowtorch (if you do not have one, preheat an overhead grill until very hot). Caramelize the sugar so that it smokes and blackens in parts. Repeat on all the slices, moving the flame around the fruit evenly and not leaving it in one area for too long – otherwise the sugar will be too bitter. Allow to cool slightly, and serve immediately.

Watermelon with lime, salt, and pepper In Thailand and Vietnam, small nuggets of tamarind meat are rolled in granulated sugar, then sprinkled with a little salt and dried chilli. This dessert has the same effect, but with slightly subtler flavours. The combination can also be used to make a refreshing drink. Using a sharp knife, cut the top and the bottom off 1 small watermelon. Remove the skin, cutting from top to bottom, so that all the skin and the white areas of flesh have been cut away. Cut each half into wedges. If you view the melon wedge from side on, it is made up of three layers. The inside, or core, layer is smooth with no seeds. Remove this layer with a small, sharp knife, and cut the flesh into bite-size chunks. Next, remove the second layer of seeds entirely. Cut the last, seed-free layer into bite-sized chunks. Chill the diced watermelon for at least 1 hour. When ready to serve, juice 2 fresh limes and add to the melon. Season well with plenty of freshly ground black pepper and a good seasoning of salt. Do not be shy with these two flavourings. Mix together and taste – you will be pleasantly surprised. Serves 4–6.

Serves 4–6

1 fresh pineapple

100g (3½oz) yellow rock sugar (available from Chinese supermarkets) or crystallized coffee sugar

½ teaspoon dried red chilli flakes

Partner with
Marinated grilled mackerel (pp22–3)
Spiced prawn cakes on sticks of lemongrass (pp34–5)

Goash-e-feel | Elephant ear pastries

You can make these great pastries large or small. The name comes from the shape that the sweet pastry forms when it is fried, rather than the size – or, indeed, the origin. There are many variations of how they are finished. They can be drizzled with a scented syrup made with orange flower water or rose water, or dusted with sugar and spices, or sprinkled with icing sugar and ground pistachio nuts. *Goash-e-feel* are made all across once what was the vast Persian empire, so they may be found in Iran, Pakistan, Turkey, and Afghanistan.

Makes 16 small ones or 8 large
1 egg
1 tablespoon butter, melted
100ml (3½fl oz) milk
225g (8oz) plain flour
pinch of salt
1 teaspoon icing sugar
vegetable oil for shallow-frying

For the topping
30g (1oz) pistachio nuts
50g (1¾oz) icing sugar
2 teaspoons ground cinnamon

Partner with
Potato and cauliflower
pakoras (pp66–7)
Gujarati aubergine fritters
(pp82–3)

1 Beat the egg in a bowl, and add the melted butter. Add just enough of the milk to make the liquid up to 110ml (4fl oz). Sift in the flour with a pinch of salt and the icing sugar. Add to the egg and milk mixture, and mix to form a firm dough. Knead the dough on a lightly floured surface for 8–10 minutes until smooth and elastic. Roll into 16 small (or 8 large) balls, place on a lightly floured baking sheet, and leave to rest under a damp cloth for about 40 minutes.

2 On a lightly floured work surface, roll out each ball into a circle so that it is as thin as possible and as wide as possible. Using your fingers and thumb, pleat one half of each pastry disc, then nip together with dampened fingers so that the pleat holds together while the pastries are frying. To make the topping, grind the pistachio nuts until fine; mix the icing sugar and cinnamon together. Have ready for when the pastries come out of the hot oil.

3 In a large frying pan, heat enough oil for shallow-frying over a medium-high heat. When the oil is hot, put in the pastries one or two at a time, depending on the pan's size. Fry for 1½–2 minutes on each side until golden. Remove the ears from the pan with a slotted spoon, carefully shaking off any excess oil. Drain on kitchen paper.

4 Allow the pastries to cool a little, then sprinkle first with the icing sugar mixture, then the ground pistachio nuts. Serve warm or cold. You could also make smaller versions of these pastries by forming small bowtie shapes.

Pomegranate and blood orange fruit salad

Over the winter, one of the highlights of what can otherwise seem a bleak time of the year is the bounty of citrus fruits. In this brightly coloured winter fruit salad, blood oranges and pomegranates are spiked with eastern spices. Like many fruit dishes from Central Asia, it feels indulgent and exotic, but is very cleansing and refreshing.

Serves 4–6

4 blood oranges or juicy
  navel oranges

4 mandarin oranges

2 pomegranates

1 teaspoon runny honey

2 green cardamom pods

1 teaspoon ground cinnamon or
  1 cinnamon stick

100g (3½oz) peeled unsalted
  pistachio nuts, roughly
  chopped

Partner with
Minced pork balls with
garlic and pepper (pp38–9)
Sichuan chicken
dumplings (p100)

1 With a sharp knife, remove the peel and pith from the blood or navel oranges and the mandarins. Over a small non-corrosive saucepan, segment an orange using the sharp knife, by cutting just inside the dividing membrane of the segments. Save any juice in the pan. When all the segments are divided, squeeze the remaining pith and membrane to extract all the juice possible. Repeat with all the fruit. Put the orange segments in a bowl and set aside.

2 To deseed the pomegranate, first take the whole fruit in your hand and, using a wooden spoon, tap it firmly all over about 20 times. This loosens the seeds inside so that they can be removed. Cut the fruit in half with a sharp knife (there will be a lot of juice to add to the pan of orange juice). Over a bowl, again tap the halved fruit on the skin with a wooden spoon, so that all the seeds fall out and the bitter white pith is left behind.

3 Add the runny honey to the pan of juices. With the back of a knife or a wooden spoon, crush the cardamom pods to release the central seeds that contain the oils. Discard the husks, and add the seeds to the pan. Sprinkle in the ground cinnamon or add the cinnamon stick (this is removed before serving). Stir to incorporate all the ingredients. Bring the citrus juices and spices to the boil, and simmer for 1 minute. Remove from the heat and set the liquid aside to allow to cool and for the flavours to infuse.

4 When cool, pour over the segmented citrus fruit. Mix together with the pomegranate seeds. Chill until needed. To serve, scatter the pistachio nuts over the marinated fruit, and serve as a light and colourful end to a meal or with Greek-style yoghurt, crème fraîche, or ice cream, or to moisten a Mediterranean orange cake.

Pear fritters with cinnamon honey syrup

A simple dessert that could be eaten as a snack with refreshing drinks. You could alter the aromatic element that goes into the syrup using different dried spices or vanilla or ginger. A few sprigs of rosemary could also be used – this makes a delicious syrup to go with apples, pears, or quince.

1 To make the honey and cinnamon syrup, combine the honey and wine (and sugar, if using) in a pan. Simmer for 3–4 minutes with the cinnamon sticks until slightly reduced, then leave to cool.

2 Next make the batter. Whisk together the egg yolks, wine, milk, and olive oil, then slowly add the flour, whisking all the time until the batter is smooth. In a clean bowl, whisk the egg whites until they form soft peaks. Stir one third of the egg white into the flour mixture to loosen, then gently fold in the remaining egg white.

3 Heat the oil in a deep saucepan until hot but not smoking – a splash of batter should sizzle straight away. Peel, halve, and core the pears, then cut each pear half into six slices lengthways.

4 Cook the fritters in batches, to keep the temperature of the oil from dropping too much and ensure that your fritters are crisp. Dip the pear slices into the batter, allowing any excess to drain off. Deep-fry the battered pears for 4 minutes or until golden and puffed, turning once during the cooking time. Drain on kitchen paper, and keep warm in the bottom of the oven while you are cooking the remaining fritters. Repeat the process until all the pear slices have been used. Serve immediately, with the honey and cinnamon syrup drizzled over the fritters.

Serves 6

light vegetable oil for deep-frying

4 ripe pears such as Williams or Comice

For the cinnamon honey syrup

3 tablespoons honey

60ml (2fl oz) sweet white wine such as Vin Santo or Muscat*

2 cinnamon sticks

For the batter

2 eggs, separated

125ml (4fl oz) sweet white wine*

125ml (4fl oz) milk

2 tablespoons extra virgin olive oil

125g (4½oz) flour

* If sweet wine is not available, use white wine with 1½ tablespoons caster sugar.

Partner with
Chinese barbecue spare ribs (pp24–5)
Pork and cabbage dumplings (p75)

Kaymakli kurk kayisi | Stuffed apricots

Apricots were orginally native to China, but their gradual spread through trade means that they are now found across Asia, as well as other parts of the world. These stuffed apricots make a delicious snack that can be eaten at any time, either with coffee or as a part of a larger dessert selection. You could also use figs or dates for this dish. It is simple to make, but very impressive to guests. Always buy the plumpest dried fruits available, rather than ones that are over-dried and shrivelled.

Serves 6

450g dried apricots or dates

200g (7oz) sugar

3 green cardamom pods

1 cinnamon stick

2 cloves

juice of ½ lemon

3 tablespoons mascarpone cheese or clotted cream

30g (1oz) skinless pistachio nuts, finely ground

1 Put the dried fruit in a bowl, cover with water, and soak overnight until they are swollen and softened. The next day, remove the apricots or dates from the liquid using a slotted spoon, and set aside. Top up the soaking liquid with water to make it up to 600ml (1 pint).

2 Pour the liquid into a pan, and add the sugar, cardamom, cinnamon, and cloves. Slowly bring to the boil to dissolve the sugar. Simmer for 10 minutes, then add the soaked apricots. Simmer the apricots for another 10 minutes until they have softened and the liquid has become syrupy. Add the lemon juice and cook for a further minute. Remove from the heat, and take out the apricots using a slotted spoon. Allow both the apricots and the syrup to cool.

3 Mix the mascarpone or cream with 3 tablespoons of the cooled apricot syrup. When the apricots have cooled, split them in half and fill with the mascarpone mxiture. Sprinkle the ground pistachio nuts over the top, and serve.

Partner with
Lamb pilaf with saffron
and nuts (p104)
Spiced stuffed aubergine (p165)
Elephant ear pastries (pp196–7)

Keynotes | **Aromatic spices**

The potent alchemy of spices of the East conjure up images of ancient trade routes, riches, intrigue, and mystery. Wars have been waged and conquests made over these bounteous aromatics. Spices were

> "These spices were Asia's best and most valuable export long before people in the West knew what the people of these lands looked like or what other foods they ate."

Asia's best and most valuable export long before people in the West knew what the people of these lands looked like or what other foods they ate.

Spices became popular for their flavour and the sense of grandeur they gave to food. They were also widely used in pickling and preserving, and to mask the intense flavour of putrid and spoiled food. At one time, salt for preserving was expensive; cold weather was the only other main food preservation method. In Elizabethan times, spices were more widely used in a kitchen than today for this reason. For some, the aromas of these spices often create an image of Christmas. Cured hams are often still studded with cloves. Mince pies, plum pudding, Christmas pudding, Christmas cake – all contain spices that in earlier times were added to the fruits after the autumnal harvest.

Another important factor in the use of spices in preserving is the antiseptic qualities found in a number of them. The oils in cinnamon, cloves, ginger, white mustard seeds, aniseed, juniper, and pepper are all powerful preservatives.

Cinnamon

Cinnamon (*Cinnamomum verum*) has a distinctive smell that is warm, sweet, and comforting. The cinnamon quills come from the inner bark of an evergreen camphor laurel that is related to the bay tree. Originally native to Sri Lanka, but now grown in China and all over Asia, as well as on the Caribbean "spice" island of Grenada, cinnamon is widely used in the cuisines of India, Vietnam, Morocco, Iran, and Malaysia, in both savoury and sweet dishes. The powdered form, though convenient, is inferior to the cinnamon quills because it goes stale and loses its flavour. The best way to use any spice is whole; if you need ground spice, grind it yourself.

Star anise

Star anise (*Illicium verum*) is a star-shaped seed pod; its intrigue lies in its beauty and also its incredibly intense taste. It has much more robust aniseed and licorice-like flavours than regular anise seeds, and works well with braises and slow-cooked dishes. Star anise is one of the main ingredients of Chinese five-spice and so is present in the very air that you breathe in any Chinatown or Chinese community around the world. In Europe, the popularity of this jewel of a spice dates back to the 16th century. The famous Vietnamese soup called *pho*, a name which comes from the French *pot au feu* ("pot on the fire"), has an intense stock perfumed with star anise, cinnamon, and ginger.

Cassia

Although cassia (*Cinnamomum burmannii*) is similar to cinnamon and has a similar fragrance, the two should not be confused. Cassia is the bark of a related tree native to the northeast Indian state of Assam and to Burma; the part used as a spice is the outer bark. It has a much more robust and pronounced aroma than cinnamon. Favoured in Indian, Burmese, Vietnamese, and Chinese cuisines, its toughness makes it harder to grind, so either leave whole or use some that has already been ground.

Clove

The English name for this small, highly aromatic spice is derived from the Latin word *clavus*, which means "nail". In India, cloves are sometimes used for exactly that – to fasten small paper packets. The dried unopened flower buds of a tree that comes from the myrtle family (*Syzygium aromaticum*), cloves have a very powerful flavour and should be used sparingly; their pungent taste creates a numbing sensation, which is why they are used the world over for toothache. Used in sweet and savoury dishes, cloves also feature in spice mixes such as Chinese five-spice and are used for pickling and preserving, and for their antiseptic properties. They are commonly found in Middle Eastern sweet pastries.

Cloves

Cinnamon quills

Star anise

Cardamom pods

Nutmeg

The common or fragrant nutmeg tree (*Myristica fragrans*) is indigenous to the Moluccas, and yields two different spices from the same fruit: nutmeg and mace. A warm, sweet spice, nutmeg should not be overused for two reasons: it has a strong flavour and is a potent hallucinogen. In India, nutmeg is used almost exclusively in sweet dishes and sometimes in garama masala. In the Middle East, nutmeg is often used for savoury dishes, while Japanese varieties of curry powder include nutmeg.

Mangosteen, lychee, and mango salad

Mangosteens are a delicious Asian fruit available from good greengrocers and Chinese and Thai food stores. They have a dark, hard skin that gives nothing away of the tempting flesh that is inside. The flesh is white and has the extraordinary taste of a combination of wild strawberries, bananas, and citrus. Mangosteens are a definitely worth seeking out if you have never had one before. If not available, use some sliced bananas – they have a similar flavour and texture. Other combinations of Asian fruits, such as pineapple and papaya, also work well.

Serves 4–6

4 kaffir lime leaves

18 lychees

2 ripe mangoes

8 mangosteens

20 fresh mint leaves

For the passion fruit dressing

4cm (1¾in) piece of fresh root ginger, finely chopped

1 tablespoon caster sugar

2 passion fruits

juice of 1 orange

juice of 1 lime

Partner with
Stir-fried beef with chilli and onion relish (p33)
Pickled daikon salad with fried garlic (p142)

1 Using a sharp knife, shave off the raised stem on the back of the kaffir lime leaves so that the leaves are flat. Tightly roll the leaves into a cigar shape. Working the knife rhythmically, finely shred the rolled lime leaves into thin slivers. Set aside.

2 With the skin still on the lychees, cut them in half through the stone, then slip off the skins and discard the stones. Peel the mango and cut the flesh into large lobes, then cut into equal-sized slices about 1cm (½in) thick. To open the mangosteens, make a horizontal cut around the middle of the fruit with a small serrated knife. Cut until the half lifts off. Be careful, as the skin is very hard, so you will have to press quite firmly. The outer pith of the fruit is red and the fruit is white. Remove and discard the hard black stones inside.

3 To make the passion fruit dressing, use a mortar and pestle to crush the ginger with the sugar, to form a smooth paste. Halve the passion fruits, and scrape the pulp into the ginger paste. Stir through, then mix with the orange and lime juice.

4 Gently mix the lychee, mango, and mangosteen in a large bowl. Sprinkle with the mint leaves and shredded lime leaves, and stir through carefully. Add the dressing and gently stir through again. Serve immediately as a refreshing end to an Asian meal.

Doogh | Yoghurt and mint drink

Many variations of this is very refreshing drink with ancient origins are found across Asia, from what was the Persian empire through to the Indian subcontinent. Some variations are sweet, while others are more salty and sour. What they all have in common is that they pick you up when faced with too much heat. *Doogh* is a truly thirst-quenching drink that has a long-lasting effect. You can use ice cubes or crushed ice, or simply serve chilled from the refrigerator.

1 Whisk together the yoghurt and soured cream with the lemon juice and salt until smoothly blended. Add the cucumber and mint, and stir through to mix.

2 Pour in 1 litre (1¾ pints) water, and mix together so that it does not separate. Keep in the refrigerator, ready to use, until you need this thirst-quencher. The combination of salt and acidity works to be very refreshing, in the same way as a modern icotonic drink combines important salts and minerals, as well as sugars, to revive you when you are dehydrated.

Serves 4–6

500g (1lb 2oz) Greek-style yoghurt

75g (2½oz) soured cream

juice of 1 lemon

1 tablespoon salt

1 small Lebanese cucumber, peeled and grated

3 sprigs of fresh mint, leaves picked and roughly chopped

Partner with
Burmese turmeric fishcakes (p80)
Potatoes with turmeric and mustard seeds (pp174–5)

Bastani sa labi | Saffron ice cream with pistachio nuts

Persian ice cream is famed for how irresistible it is. Richly perfumed with rose water, saffron, and pistachio nuts, this simple ice cream has a very decadent look. There is also an interesting textural note to Persian ice cream. Just before the end of the freezing process, small chips of frozen double cream are stirred into the ice cream. When the ice cream is eaten, these chewy pieces provide a contrast to the creamy texture of the rest of the tempting dessert.

Serves 4

500ml (16fl oz) milk

250g (9oz) caster sugar

3 tablespoons Greek-style yoghurt

2 teaspoons rose water

1 teaspoon saffron threads, soaked in 2 tablespoons boiling milk

2 tablespoons frozen chips of double cream, to be added at the end of freezing

3 tablespoons chopped pistachio nuts

1 Bring the milk to the boil over a medium-high heat, then remove the pan from the heat. Beat the yoghurt and sugar together until all the sugar has dissolved. Whisk in the milk, then add the rose water and the saffron and its liquid.

2 Pour into the ice-cream machine, and freeze and churn for 30 minutes according to the manufacturer's instructions. (If you do not have an ice-cream maker, then it simply involves a bit more effort. Every 10 minutes, remove the ice cream from the freezer and whisk for a couple of minutes, then return to the freezer once more.)

3 Five minutes before the end of the freezing process, remove the frozen double cream from the freezer, and chop into small nuggets. Add the nuggets to the churning ice cream. When the ice cream is softly firm, scoop into a chilled bowl or individual bowls, and keep covered in the freezer until you need it.

4 To serve, garnish the golden ice cream with the pistachio nuts. Serve as an accompaniment to roasted fruits or cakes such as the Yoghurt and Pistachio Cake on pp186–7.

Partner with
Afghan caramelized quince compote (p190)
Afghan new year compote (p191)

Menu ideas

Part of the pleasure of experiencing food from other parts of the world is learning to mix and match flavours and food styles. The menus that follow are designed to help you on your way, so that you can take yourself on a tasting journey through the various cuisines. They are a guide only, so feel free to experiment as you please. Sampling different taste sensations in a single meal is an excellent way to whet your appetite for more. An added bonus is that these recipes all work well for entertaining – impress your guests with your culinary repertoire.

Menu 1

◁ Stir-fried greens with garlic **Vietnam** pp18–19

Chinese barbecue spare ribs **China** pp24–5

Tamarind fried prawns **Malaysia** pp154–5

Spring onion and chive flower rolls **China** pp110–11

Grilled aubergine salad **Burma** pp128–9

Menu 2

◁ Marinated grilled mackerel **Indonesia** pp22–3

Pork and cabbage dumplings **Korea** p75

Crisp cabbage salad with peanuts **Laos** pp134–5

Fresh coconut chutney **Singapore** p133

Crisp peanut wafers **Indonesia** p65

Watermelon with lime, salt, and pepper **Modern Asian** p195

Menu 3

◁ Steamed prawn wontons **China** pp98–9

Seared scallops with fresh chutney **India** pp16–17

Grilled beef patties with shallots and cumin **Vietnam** pp26–7

Spring onion pancakes **Korea** pp60–1

Nonya bean curd salad **Singapore** pp136–7

Menu 4

◁ Burmese spiced split pea fritters **Burma** pp90–1

Isaan-style grilled chicken **Thailand** pp40–1

Spiced prawn cakes on sticks of lemongrass **Vietnam** pp34–5

Fried bean sprouts and clams **Malaysia** pp94–5

Potato with turmeric and mustard seeds **Singapore** pp174–5

Menu 5

◁ Sesame chicken salad with white pepper **China** pp118–19
Nonya-style spicy pork **Singapore** pp114–15
Curried sweetcorn fritters **Thailand** pp70–1
Carrot pachadi **India** pp162–3
Garlic and coriander naan **India** p49
Pear fritters with cinnamon honey syrup **Iran** pp202–3

Menu 6

◁ Marinated barbecue beef **Korea** pp52–3
Korean hot pickled cabbage **Korea** p164
North Vietnamese fish brochettes **Vietnam** pp46–7
Mushroom pot-sticker dumplings **China** pp106–7
Tomato chutney with green chilli **India** p179

Menu 7

◁ Keralan spiced chickpea and lentil dumplings **India** pp56–7
Miso soup with seven-spice chicken **Japan** pp96–7
Indonesian fried rice **Indonesia** p32
Stir-fried beef with chilli and onion relish **Thailand** p33
Pickled daikon salad with fried garlic **Burma** p142

Menu 8

◁ Potato and cauliflower pakoras **Afghanistan** pp 66–7
Sardines with green chilli sambal **Malaysia** pp44–5
Sichuan chicken dumplings **China** p100
Cured prawns with shredded lime leaves **Thailand** p123
Mangosteen, lychee, and mango salad **Modern Asian** p208

Menu 9

◁ Gujarati aubergine fritters **India** pp82–3

Sumatran minced duck sate **Indonesia** pp50–1

Sesame tempura **Japan** pp78–9

Sichuan peppered beef **China** pp170–1

Stir-fried bean sprouts with hot red bean paste **Korea** p21

Menu 10

◁ Malay beef rendang **Malaysia** pp148–9

Minced pork balls with garlic and pepper **Vietnam** pp38–9

Steamed green vegetable rolls **Korea** p106

Sri Lankan smoky aubergine dip **Sri Lanka** pp150–1

Rice flour pancakes **Sri Lanka** p81

Citrus and young coconut jelly **Thailand** pp184–5

Menu 11

◁ Hot and sour green papaya salad **Thailand** pp144–5

Tamarind beef with peanuts **Vietnam** pp180–1

Malaysian fried noodles **Malaysia** p20

Prawn and chive spring rolls **China** pp72–3

Chilled seared tuna with ginger **Japan** pp120–1

Menu 12

◁ Pineapple with caramelized chilli **Modern Asian** pp194–5

Fresh lettuce cups with chicken **China** pp124–5

Singapore coconut laksa **Singapore** p112

Roast pork with fresh mint and peanuts **Vietnam** pp158–9

Laotian spice-pickled spring onions **Laos** pp168–9

Menu 13

◁ Asian salad with pea shoots and sprouts **Modern Asian** pp140–1

Spicy lamb-stuffed pancakes **Singapore** p74

Happy crêpes **Vietnam** pp86–7

Sashimi of sea bream with hot dressing **Korea** p143

Sumatran aubergine sambal **Indonesia** pp88–9

Menu 14

◁ Spicy apricot chutney **Afghanistan** pp160–1

Lamb pilaf with saffron and nuts **Pakistan** p104

Spiced stuffed aubergine **Turkey** p165

Fried puffed potato bread **India** pp62–3

Afghan new year compote **Afghanistan** p191

Menu 15

◁ Fried squid flowers with ginger and spices **China** pp58–9

Burmese turmeric fishcakes **Burma** p80

Steamed barbecue pork buns **China** p101

Spicy green beans with chilli **Singapore** pp30–1

Fried aubergine with toasted sesame seeds **Korea** p178

Menu 16

◁ Chilled soba noodles with seared salmon **Japan** pp130–1

Nonya pork, prawn, and crab ball soup **Malaysia** p113

Lemon and saffron chicken kebabs **Iran** pp172–3

Spring onion and chive flower rolls **China** pp110–11

Pomegranate and blood orange fruit salad **Iran** pp200–1

Glossary

agar agar A natural setting agent used in Asia (sometimes known as *kanten*), agar agar is derived from seaweed; it comes in blocks, as a powder, or in strands, and can be found in Thai and other Asian grocers and health-food shops. If unavailable, substitute with gelatine leaves or powdered gelatine (agar agar sets more easily, so you may need to adjust amounts).

asafoetida powder Ground from a plant that is similar to fennel, asafoetida powder has an extremely pungent garlic-like smell and should be used sparingly. Found mostly in Indian cooking, it is a flavour enhancer. It can be found in Indian grocers.

bok choy Part of the Brassica family, bok choy is also known as Chinese white cabbage and white mustard cabbage. It is used in salad and stir-fries.

Chinese cabbage Also called napa cabbage, celery cabbage, and Peking cabbage, Chinese cabbage is part of the mustard family. Not to be confused with bok choy, it is used in salads and stir-fries.

choi sum Another member of the cabbage family, this is also called flowering white cabbage and Chinese flowering cabbage. Choi sum is used in salads and stir-fries, and is available from Asian and Chinese grocers, and better greengrocers.

daikon Also known as mooli, Japanese radish, Chinese radish, or Oriental radish, this long root vegetable has crisp white flesh; the skin is either creamy white or black. Look for daikon with unwrinkled skin. Daikon can be used raw in salads or as a garnish, or cooked in stir-fries. It is available from Indian, Asian, and Japanese grocers.

dashi Dashi is a Japanese stock made with *katsuobushi* (dried bonito flakes) and *kombu* (dried kelp seaweed).

fish sauce This pungent liquid made from fermented anchovies or other fish is an essential Southeast Asian ingredient. Its loses its fishiness on cooking, mellowing to add flavour. Recipes for this vary, but can be used interchangeably. Known as *nam pla* in Thailand and *nuoc nam* in Vietnam, it is available from good supermarkets and Asian grocers.

galangal Especially popular in Thai cuisine, galangal is a hot and peppery aromatic rhizome. A little like ginger root, it is used as a seasoning throughout Southeast Asia. Galangal is available in both root and dried form from Asian grocers.

ketjap manis Favoured in Indonesia, ketjap (or kecap) manis is similar to soy sauce, but is sweetened with palm sugar and contains seasonings such as star anise and garlic. It is can be found at Southeast Asian grocers and Chinese supermarkets.

kochujang Also known as kochu chang, this is a fiery red paste from Korea that is made from fermented soya or black beans and red chilli. Sunchang kochujang comes from the region of the same name, where it is a speciality. Deliciously addictive, it is available from Asian grocers and supermarkets.

kombu Commonly used in Japanese cooking, kombu is |kelp seaweed that has been dried in the sun before being folded into sheets. Kombu is used in combination with dried bonito flakes for the Japanese stock *dashi*, as well as for sushi and other dishes. The sun-dried kelp acts as a flavour enhancer. It was from kelp that the Japanese first extracted monosodium glutamate (MSG). Kombu is available from Japanese and Asian grocers, as well as some health-food shops.

palm sugar Made from the sap of date or coconut palms, this is also known as coconut sugar, gur, and jaggery. In India, the term *jaggery* also refers to sugar refined from raw sugarcane.

rock sugar A type of Chinese sugar, rock sugar is crystallized in large chunks, which then need to be broken up for use in cooking. It is not as sweet as ordinary granulated sugar and can be found at Asian grocers and Chinese supermarkets.

sambal oelek A sambal is a spicy and fiery paste made from primarily from chillies, which is served as a condiment. Sambal oelek is perhaps the most basic type, made with chillies, brown sugar, and salt. It is available in jars from Asian grocers.

Shaoxing rice wine Rice wine is made by fermenting glutinous rice or millet. In China, Shaoxing rice wine, from the province of Zheijang, is considered to be the finest. Make sure you buy true rice wine from a Chinese supermarket or Asian food store; if unavailable, substitute with a good-quality dry sherry.

shichimi togarashi Also known as Japanese seven-spice, shichimi togarashi (see p69) is available from Japanese and Asian grocers. It can be sprinkled over udon noodles or on fish or meat before cooking.

shrimp paste This is made from salted fermented prawns, and recipes vary slightly depending on where it is made. It should be used only sparingly and is available from Asian grocers.

sour cherry The sour cherry (*Prunus cerasus*) is smaller than its sweet counterpart; there are several varieties, including Aleppo, Montmorency, and Morello. Fresh sour cherries are usually available from late spring to early summer. Fresh Aleppo sour cherries can be difficult to come by unless you have a good Middle Eastern grocer nearby. Dried sour cherries are a perfect substitute and are available from good supermarkets.

tamarind An essential ingredient in Indian and Southeast Asian cooking, tamarind is also found in Middle Eastern and Persian recipes. The fruit of the tamarind are large pods yielding both seeds and a tart pulp. Used as a flavouring in much the same way as lemon juice, the pulp comes in concentrated form in jars, as a paste, in a dried brick, or as a powder. It is available from Indian, Asian, and some Middle Eastern grocers.

Thai basil See p139. If Thai basil is not available, substitute a combination of fresh coriander and mint leaves.

Vietnamese mint See p139.

young coconut Young coconut is available shredded and frozen in its sweet water from Chinese, Thai, and Indian food stores. It is also available in cans, but the frozen alternative is better.

Useful websites

India and Sri Lanka
www.indianspiceshop.com
www.memsaab.co.uk
www.pureindianspices.co.uk
www.spicesofindia.co.uk
www.tamleni.com
www.hindustan.com.au

Japan and Korea
www.japancentre.com
www.japanesekitchen.co.uk
www.mountfuji.co.uk
www.orientalmart.co.uk

China and Southeast Asia
www.loonfung.co.uk
www.taladthai.co.uk
www.theasiancookshop.co.uk
www.wingyip.com
www.asianfoods.com.au
www.tqc-burlington.com.au

Central and Western Asia
www.belazu.com
www.seasonedpioneers.co.uk

General
www.hardtofindfoods.co.uk
www.thespiceshop.co.uk
www.gourmetshopper.com.au

Index

Acknowledgments

Author's acknowledgment

Thank you to Mary-Clare Jerram, Carl Raymond, and Monika Schlitzer for seeing the potential in my writing; to Borra Garson and Lauren Davies at Deborah McKenna Ltd. Thank you to Dawn Henderson, Siobhán O'Connor, Susan Downing, and Simon Daley and the fantastic teams at DK in London, New York, and Germany. To everyone at Penguin in Australia for their help and support.

Thank you to Lisa Linder, for capturing the true essence of my food on film, and to her assistant Julia Kepinska. Thanks to Alice Hart for styling the food so beautifully.

Huge appreciation to the people from around the world who so generously helped in my pursuit of this book. First, Heather Paterson who makes my life work. To Tim Kemp for the fantastic opportunities in London and New York. In Malta, big thanks to Michael Zammit Tobana, owner of the Fortina Spa Resort; to the chefs at Taste, at the Fortina, who cook my food so well.

To the great cooks who have inspired me: Rose Gray and Ruth Rogers at the River Café, Rick Stein, Loyd Grossman, Peter Doyle from Est in Sydney, David Thompson.

To Tim Lee and Ashley Huntington, for keeping the debate on food wide open; Bernie Plaisted, for being my best man in the kitchen; Danielle and Rafael Fox Brinner, Kifah Arif, JJ Holland, Charlie Mash, Sarah Rowden, Clare Kelly, Birgit Erath, and Celia Brooks Brown. Thank you to the people who support my career: Chantal Rutherford Brown, the Cutting Edge School of Food and Wine, Books for Cooks, Susan Pieterse, Tertia Goodwin, everyone at Leiths, Liz Trigg, Toby Peters, Peter Durose, Helen Chislet, Jaimin and Amandip Kotecha, Hugh and Celina Arnold, Gail Arnold and Howard Crump.

To Tasting Australia, Matt Maddocks, Wye Yap, Peter Harman, Susan Foster, Chris Pinzone, and everyone in Sydney. To Debbie Wallen, Annette Peters, Helena Fleming, Caroline Crumby at Marks and Spencer. To all the chefs and friends who make it so much fun. This book is for you.

Publisher's acknowledgment

Dorling Kindersley would like to thank Simon Daley and Siobhán O'Connor for being a joy to work with when the pressure is on, Andrew Roff for extra editorial assistance and Hilary Bird for producing the index.

Picture credits

The publisher would like to thank the following for their kind permission to reproduce their photographs:

Alamy Images: Melvyn Longhurst 212; Jon Arnold: 37, 108; Corbis: Krishnendu Halder/Reuters 146; Getty Images: Neil Emmerson 14; Frans Lemmens 199; David Noton 82; Anthony Plummer 166; Hugh Sitton 167; Keren Su 54, 116; VEER Steven Puetzer 126; Jochem D Wijnands 76; Lonely Planet Images: John Banagan 127; Photolibrary: Botanica 182; Photoshot: Joan Swinnerton 109; Rex Features: 36; Robert Harding Picture Library: Yadid Levy 198; Still Pictures: M. Lohmann 77

All other images © Dorling Kindersley
For further information see: www.dkimages.com